Political Theory

Political Theory:
Tradition and Interpretation

JOHN G. GUNNELL

State University of New York at Albany

Winthrop Publishers, Inc.   Cambridge, Massachusetts

Library of Congress Cataloging in Publication Data

Gunnell, John G
    Political theory.

    Includes bibliographical references and index.
    1.   Political science—History.   I.   Title.
JA81.G93   320'.09   78–14495
ISBN 0-87626-713-4

Photo Credits

Cover photo courtesy of the Bodleian Library, Oxford, MS Ashm 304, fol. 31
Page 2, page 64, The Bettman Archive
Page 32, copyright of the National Galleries of Scotland
Page 94, copyright of the National Portrait Gallery, London

Cover design by Ann Washer

Photo research by Carole Frohlich

© *1979 by Winthrop Publishers, Inc.*
    17 Dunster Street, Cambridge, Massachusetts 02138

10   9   8   7   6   5   4   3   2   1

For Dede

Contents

Preface

Theory and practice.—Fateful distinction . . .

Nietzsche

In some instances, competent practice, or knowledge of how to perform in an activity, precedes and is quite distinct from theories or knowledge about that practice. Certainly, for example, the natural sciences, as a collection of activities, preceded and are clearly differentiated from academic philosophy of science and its attempt to give an account of the methodological principles common to these enterprises. Natural science, for the most part, has not been particularly concerned with systematic reflection on the character of its own endeavors, and it has not been notably aware of, or affected by, discussions of its activity by philosophers and historians of science. The human studies, on the other hand, are traditionally more reflective, and here practice and the theory of that practice tend to have a more integral relationship. This is certainly the case with social science. The philosophy of the social sciences concerns itself with analyzing, and making recommendations about, the practice of social scientific inquiry, and social scientists are not only influenced by such discussions but spend a great deal of time considering similar issues and reflecting upon the character of their activity. It is very difficult to specify definite boundaries between the theory and practice of social science or between social science and the philosophy of social science. This mutual relationship between theory and practice is even more pronounced in the history of political theory as a field of study, since, for the most part, the field is not the object of any separate philosophical discipline. The relationship is also reflected in this particular book. It is about teaching and research in the history of political theory, but it is largely the outgrowth of the practice of those activities. That practice has, in turn, been continually informed, and transformed, by reflection on and confrontation with arguments about what teaching and scholarship in this field are and should be.

Some of my greatest debts are to those very individuals whose arguments about the tradition of political theory are critically examined in this volume. I was intellectually nurtured on the works of George Sabine, Leo Strauss, Sheldon Wolin, Eric Voegelin, and Hannah Arendt, and the weaning process has been slow and incomplete. By the end of my graduate student days, I had become concerned about the extent to which philosophical assessments of contemporary politics were cast in terms of claims about the meaning of what was assumed to be *the* tradition of political theory and about the degree to which the study of the history of political theory was predicated on assumptions about the overall structure of that tradition. However, like most students of my generation, I still accepted the tradition of Western political theory as a reality and assumed that the interpretation of a classic work in this field required locating it within that tradition. My rejection of the idea of the tradition grew out of the problem of attempting to understand the classic texts in terms of that idea, and the very fact that tradition and interpretation are the focus of this study is the residue of that problem.

I am indebted to numerous classes of undergraduates for allowing me to indulge in the excitement of teaching political theory and for responding to this material with excitement. A number of graduate students have listened to my attempts to articulate some of the arguments in this book and have helped me to work through and refine them. Special thanks are due to James Unger and Richard Hurley and particularly to Norman Bowen and Donald Wrighton whose own research is reflected in Chapters I and II respectively. I wish to thank George Kateb for a number of things including a reading of portions of the first draft of the manuscript (and a couple of Chinese dinners). Robert Grady's comments on parts of the first draft were also very helpful. William Bluhm commented on an early draft, and Isaac Kramnick reviewed both the first draft and the final manuscript. James Unger undertook a line-by-line reading of the final draft and aided me in clarifying a number of ideas as well as finding the proper language to fit those ideas.

Above all I must acknowledge, and indeed celebrate, the association with my friend Charles Tarlton over the past decade. His contribution to this book, both in terms of perspicacious criticism and substantive ideas, has been considerable but yet difficult to specify precisely. My thoughts about political theory have become so entwined with his that it would be quite impossible for me to factor out what legitimately belongs to whom. Consequently, although he surely deserves some credit for whatever merit the work may possess, he can hardly be absolved of responsibility for any defects the arguments may contain.

Finally, it is a pleasure to be able to thank Maxine Morman and the secretarial staff of the Graduate School of Public Affairs at the State University of New York at Albany for their efficient and friendly aid and an occasional glass of wine. Special mention must be made of Addie Napolitano who typed the final manuscript with care and good cheer.

John G. Gunnell
Albany, New York

Introduction

I want to learn from him what is the scope of his art
and just what he professes and teaches.

Plato

PURPOSE AND AUDIENCE

This book is an introduction to the history of political theory* as a field of study. The history of political theory refers both to a subject matter and to the investigation and teaching of that subject matter, and consequently, as an introduction, this book is concerned with both the object and the mode of inquiry as well as the relationship between them. The book is designed to be appropriate for classroom use, but it does not follow the customary pattern of textbooks in this field. Although it is concerned with questions about how to approach the series of classic works (extending at least from Plato to Marx) that have conventionally constituted the subject matter of this field, it is not a survey or analysis of the content of those works and it is in no way intended as a substitute for a firsthand encounter with the primary sources themselves. The purpose is to provide a basis for that encounter. Textbooks in the history of political theory have characteristically consisted of accounts of, and commentaries on, the classic works, and they have been intended to be read in place of, or in conjunction with, these works or selections from them. In most colleges and universities, there is a distinct trend away from courses structured around such textbooks and toward courses that introduce students to the original sources which are now easily available in economical editions. There is increasing awareness that not only are undergraduates quite capable of confronting these books directly but that much of the value and excitement of this material depends on such a confrontation.

* "Political theory" is used here rather than the other common designations "political philosophy" or "political thought" largely because it seems to avoid the narrow connotation of the former and the very broad signification of the latter.

The traditional textbooks, either explicitly or implicitly, answered certain basic questions about the selection of the works studied, how they related to one another, the reasons for studying them, their meaning and significance, and their relevance for the present. But they also often tended not only to prejudice the interpretation of these works by providing a prefabricated perspective but to foreclose an exploration of these questions and to inhibit reflection on the nature of the very study in which students were engaged. For example, in most instances students and faculty had very little idea of the origins and evolution of this field, its relationship to the discipline of political science, and a whole range of issues and assumptions that had considerable eventual import for decisions about what students would be exposed to and how they would be introduced to it. The decline of the survey text as a substitute for or complement to a study of the classics may create a situation in which the material can be approached in a more critical and analytical manner, but the questions that those texts at least tacitly, but often unreflectively, answered do not disappear. This book is an attempt to make some of those questions explicit and to do so in the context of a consideration of the development of the history of political theory as a field of study and the problems that attend both research and teaching in this area. This involves certain assumptions about the relevance of these issues to the undergraduate classroom.

When I was an undergraduate, I took an introductory course in geology that, for heuristic reasons, was organized around a study of the stratigraphy of the Grand Canyon. We discussed the Kaibab limestone, the Coconino sandstone, and other layers of sedimentary rock exposed by the chasm, but when we encountered a black bedrock at the bottom of the gorge, the instructor informed us that we would not discuss that formation in Geology I and II. This was in part a strategy to encourage students to take more advanced courses, but it was also based on the assumption that knowledge must be revealed in a graduated manner. I believe that, to some extent, I initially chose geology as a major in order to determine the composition of the mysterious black rock (which turned out to be Archean schist and gneiss formed in the Precambrian period by the intrusion of igneous rock and the metamorphosis of existing sedimentary strata). I found that there was nothing about this rock that was beyond the ken of undergraduates, but it did raise certain questions about which geologists were not in full agreement. What a discussion of the black rock opened up was not merely questions about certain geological "facts" but questions about the study of geology. It demonstrated very clearly that geological knowledge and the specification of the objects of geological science were inseparable from knowledge about geology as a field of study. This book is a discussion of the "black rock" of the history of political theory and the questions about this field that such a discussion entails.

Although in some branches of natural science or mathematics, there may be a certain rationale for the notion that an introduction to a subject matter must involve a limited exposure to rudimentary knowledge in the field, and even a certain amount of distortion in order to simplify the material, it is much more difficult to make a case for such a procedure in the human and social sciences. And even in the natural sciences, there may be good reasons for arguing that it is as important to introduce students to the discipline as to the subject matter of the discipline. In any event, it would be pretentious to claim that the study of the history of political theory involves problems and issues that are beyond the competence of students or that belong to a privileged body of knowledge to which only the teacher and professional scholar are privy. The result of such assumptions is to insulate the classroom from critical discussion and introduce a spurious authority. Some of the issues and problems considered in the following chapters such as those dealing with the past history of the field may be of limited and passing concern to students, but it is necessary that they have some sense of the development of the enterprise in which they have chosen to engage and of the current character of research and teaching. The idea that undergraduates in upper division courses can be presented with information about the history of political theory but that only advanced graduate students can be introduced to issues involving the "theology" of inquiry is not convincing. Although the field has been characterized by a good deal of controversy in recent years, there has not been, at any level, an excess of self-examination, and some of the problems that can be now recognized as having surrounded research and teaching in this field for the past two or three decades derive from a perpetuation of a fundamental unreflectiveness about the subject matter and how to approach it. The issues discussed in the following chapters may not be exhaustively treated, and the theme of each chapter could well be the subject of an entire course or seminar, or even a separate book. Yet the difficult character of the problems discussed is not concealed, and they are approached in a fully explicit manner with no hedging on the arguments presented and with no intention of talking down to the audience. Certainly students in political science courses are not simply taught politics anymore as if teaching political science were merely a matter of supplying facts. It is clearly recognized that the history, current structure, and procedures of inquiry in the discipline are relevant factors in evaluating the interpretation of political data. The same is true in the history of political theory. Methodological assumptions are inseparable from empirical claims.

One of the basic premises that inform this book is that it should be intelligible to anyone but that there is little that should appear gratuitous to political scientists who specialize in this field. Although the book is an introduction to the field, it is elementary only in that the issues considered are basic to research and teaching. The book is addressed to a broad audience ranging from undergraduates to scholars in the history of political theory and related fields, and care has been taken to avoid a specialized vocabulary, unless the terms have been adequately defined, and to avoid an approach that would suggest speaking to a group of initiates.

The scope of the book is also broad, and the entire work, as well as specific chapters, is intended to perform a number of functions. For example, while an important concern is to introduce students to the field and to explore a wide range of issues regarding the study of political theory, the book is organized around a central critical thesis about past scholarship and teaching which in some respects informs each chapter. The approach is in no way polemical, and an attempt is made to present a fair account of various theses and arguments that are discussed. It is hoped that the work will be stimulating and informative even if the reader disagrees with the position that is advanced about tradition and interpretation.

It probably is fair to say that in recent years there has been something of a renaissance in the study of the history of political theory. In some respects, this may seem anomalous and difficult to explain, particularly in view of the prolonged estrangement between this field and its parent discipline, political science. In other respects (as I attempt to demonstrate in Chapter I), the increased distance between the history of political theory and mainstream orthodox political science, and the subsequent dulling of the controversy between them, have contributed to the autonomy of the former and to an increased concern on the part of historians of political theory about the nature of their subject matter and how to approach it. To some degree, this renaissance can also be attributed to the fact that the students of some of the scholars who have been most influential in the field (such as those considered in Chapters II and III) have now begun to come into prominence themselves. Yet maybe equally important is the reawakening of a concern with normative inquiry in political science that has taken place as a result of recent attention to issues of public policy. Although the history of political theory may be quite far removed from social science in many respects, the growing emphasis in social science on practical issues of social relevance has suggested to some the basis of a new complementarity between modern political inquiry and traditional issues in the history of political thought. Whatever the reasons for the revitalization of this study, it is imperative that teaching and research take place in a context of critical awareness.

Chapter I presents a brief account of the development of the history of political theory as a field of study. It is an attempt to demonstrate how it emerged, why it evolved as it did, and how certain modes of teaching and scholarship came to prevail. Particular emphasis is placed on the relationship between political science and the study of the history of political theory. Although many have come to understand this relationship in terms of the controversy that developed between the political scientists who were the advocates of behavioralism (or the application to political inquiry of what they believed to be the methods of natural science) and historians of political thought (who were generally critical of that approach), the situation for the previous hundred years had been quite different. What is often neglected is the degree to which the evolution of the history of political theory as a scholarly enterprise and as the subject of textbooks and teaching took place within the context of the development of American political science. The chapter begins with a discussion of David Easton's critique of the study of the history of political theory and with an account of the ensuing controversy about the decline of political theory. This is followed by an analysis of the literature that preceded the 1950s and the legacy that it bequeathed to later work in the field. Easton, as well as later critics, failed to interpret accurately the character and purpose of this early literature. Finally, there is a preliminary discussion of some of the most recent criticism of scholarship in the field. This criticism, which has been centered around general methodological issues in the history of ideas, is taken up again in more detail in Chapter IV. The principal purpose of this initial chapter, as it relates to the basic theme of the book, is to explain the appearance and acceptance of the *idea of the tradition* as the principal paradigm of teaching and research in the field.

The second chapter presents a brief general characterization of the principal features of the idea of the tradition and the assumptions which constitute it, while the main body of the chapter consists of an account of the arguments of four historians of political theory who have been particularly influential in elaborating this idea during the past two decades. They have substantially contributed to the belief that the basic object of study in the history of political theory is an inherited pattern of thought whose basic elements are discernible in the classic works of political literature extending from Plato to the present, and that this tradition is the basic intellectual context for interpreting particular texts. The claims of Leo Strauss, Eric Voegelin, Hannah Arendt, and Sheldon Wolin are by no means exactly the same, or even based on similar philosophical assumptions, but their work, and their notions about the tradition, exhibit a number of important structural and conceptual similarities that justify treating them together, particularly since these same features are evident in the field at large. The use of the idea of the tradition by these authors as a vehicle for undertaking a critical analysis of contemporary politics has led to the *myth of the tradition* or the imposition on the framework of the classic works of an elaborate dramatic story of the rise and fall of political theory and the implications of these events for the modern age.

The purpose of the third chapter is to undertake a critical analysis of myth of the tradition, but the intent is not so much to attack this literature as to illuminate its uses and clarify precisely what kinds of arguments are being introduced and to demonstrate the difficulties that arise if the idea of the tradition is accepted literally and unreflectively. It is necessary to understand that many of the histories of political theory written from this perspective, as well as interpretations of particular works, are not so much informed by what many would consider historical motives, or an interest in understanding the past for its own sake, as by a concern with explaining and evaluating the present. My intention in this chapter is to demonstrate that while many of the writers who propagated the myth of the tradition knew quite well what they were doing, their work led to the further unreflective entrenchment of a belief in the reality of the tradition, that is, to the assumption that the conventional chronology of classic works including at least those of Plato, Aristotle, St. Augustine, St. Thomas Aquinas, Machiavelli, Hobbes, Locke, Rousseau, Hegel, and Marx, constitutes an actual historical tradition and belongs to a distinct self-defined genre. These works are assumed to be the product of a discrete activity with a recognizable temporal career, to represent the evolution of Western political ideas, and to have causative implications for understanding contemporary politics.

The somewhat instrumental and practical concerns that governed much of the past secondary literature on the history of political theory have led some recent critics to attack it as unhistorical and to recommend that the classics now be approached in a truly historical manner and studied by rigorous historical methods. Part of the difficulty with this criticism is that it often does not take account of the actual intentions of past historians of political theory and fails to recognize that to a large extent those intentions were not historical in the sense that the critics understand that term. Another problem is that what the critics take to be the criterion of historicity, although it reflects one distinct philosophical claim about this matter, is by no means unassailable. In Chapter IV, I attempt to analyze this particular notion of historicity and contrast it with another prominent but controversial position regarding the interpretation of historical texts and what understanding of past ideas involves. The purpose of this chapter is not to provide any definitive solution to the problem of the nature of understanding and interpretation in the history of ideas, which is an important issue in all humanistic studies, but only to demonstrate its relevance to the study of political theory and to clarify some of the premises about language and meaning on which different claims about historicity rest.

Assumptions about meaning and understanding, however, are not the only regulative principles that inform the study of the history of political theory. Despite the difficulties with the idea of the tradition, it did, among other things, provide a way of identifying the substantive subject matter of the history of political theory and provide a rationale for studying it. The texts that were selected for interpretation were those which were assumed to belong to the tradition, and the significance attributed to a text was largely a matter of its alleged role in this reconstructed tradition. The myth of the tradition certainly provided a compelling answer to the question of the relevance of studying the classics and the selection of works to be designated classics. A rejection of the myth of the tradition leaves these questions of *what* and *why* very much at issue. Those who attack past scholarship for its unhistorical character provide no new answers and find themselves left to rummage through the bones that once formed the skeleton of the tradition. The final chapter does not seek to provide any definitive or exhaustive reasons for what works should be studied and why, but it does attempt to demonstrate that there are numerous reasons for studying the texts that have customarily been considered classics. It also seeks to show that although political theory as an activity and product cannot be located historically and although political theory is not a profession in which the classic authors self-consciously participated, there are, retrospectively, good reasons for treating many of the classic works as a type of literature and attempting, at least analytically, to distinguish some family resemblances between these works and the individuals who produced them. This chapter attempts to develop an ideal typification of political theory as an activity and to present a profile of the political theorist, but it is stressed that these are analytical concepts and not claims about a preconstituted tradition and literary genre.

These chapters are linked together in that each one advances elements of the organizing argument about the past, present, and future of the study of the history of political theory. For the most part, however, each chapter treats a relatively distinct problem and set of issues and serves a different function. The purpose, of course, is to achieve a certain unity in diversity.

Political Theory

Machiavelli 1469–1527

I

The History of Political Theory
as a Field of Study:
Retrospect

. . . if we could but recover the point of view of the author himself, and read out of our minds for the moment the later development of institutions and ideas about them.

McIlwain

POLITICAL SCIENCE AND THE DECLINE
OF POLITICAL THEORY

The genealogy of the history of political theory as a field of study is complex. In the United States it has been closely linked with, and often an integral aspect of, the development of the discipline of political science. The relationship has not always been congenial. Although the history of political theory is recognized today as a subfield of political science, it often has been the object, as well as the source, of criticism concerning the character and direction of the discipline. To understand the current status of studies in the history of political theory, it is necessary to understand this relationship. To a large extent, it was a conflict with the dominant persuasion in political science that shaped the character of these studies during the past thirty years.

In the early 1950s the political scientists who championed the behavioral movement, or the idea of a science of politics modeled after the methodology of the natural sciences, were intent on establishing the autonomy of the discipline as an empirical science and rescuing political theory from an identification with the history of political ideas and the study of classic texts from Plato to the present. David Easton, in his classic diagnosis of the "impoverishment" of political theory, argued that political theory as practiced by Aristotle, Locke, and others in the Western tradition of political thought had given way to the history of political theory. It had been reduced to a "form of historical analysis" that lived "parasitically" on the ideas of the past, and it had relinquished its traditional role "of creatively constructing a valuational frame of reference." At the same time, it rejected the "task of building systematic theory about political behavior and the operation of political institutions" that was essential for the development of an empirical political science.[1]

From its "birth as a discipline in ancient Greece" to its end, "perhaps with Hegel and Marx," political theory had focused on "practical affairs" and the appraisal of social policy. However, Easton argued, in the twentieth century political theory had given up "analyzing and formulating new value theory" in favor of "retailing information about the meaning, internal consistency, and historical development of contemporary and past political values."[2] This decline of political theory into historicism was manifest in the work of individuals such as W. A. Dunning, C. H. McIlwain, and G. H. Sabine whose textbooks and approach to research had dominated the field since 1900. The historicist orientation, Easton charged, was the product of a tendency to accept uncritically contemporary values. An increasing consensus of values in the West had led to an intellectual climate of moral relativism and to a decline of creative value theory. Yet, he argued, moral relativism did not logically entail a retreat from value judgment, and, in an age marked by the appearance of fascism and other forms of totalitarianism, moral complacency and an abstinence from valuation was an unconscionable retreat from commitment. Easton maintained that the typical historian of political ideas was not interested in past political values in relation to the present but rather undertook "their history largely for the sake of narration."[3] Whether they saw past values as epiphenomena and rationalizations of institutions and interests, as causal elements in politics, as reflections of the prevailing culture of an age, or as explanations of the emergence of contemporary values, these historians all approached values in terms of an uncritical attempt to objectively explicate "the relation of ideas to the social environment" and to a particular historical situation.[4]

In addition to abdicating responsibility for confronting practical value problems in the present, Easton held, the approach of the historicist was also detrimental to scientific inquiry in that it "failed to provide the student of political life with the skills and knowledge necessary to explore his own moral preconceptions."[5] Since all empirical research, including problem selection and the interpretation of results, inevitably takes place within a framework of values, an awareness of, and reflection on, this framework is necessary to separate facts from values and guarantee objectivity. Furthermore, he argued, a sensitivity to values is necessary to insure that social scientific knowledge is relevant to social problems and to political decision-making.

However, in Easton's view, historicism was deficient not only in its approach to values but in its exclusive concern with values: "research in political theory is now equated with the study of value theory."[6] Easton maintained that traditional political theory had been concerned with facts as well as values. It was grounded on descriptive and practical propositions about politics and political change that implied "a generalized causal theory about the relations of facts."[7] Although it had failed to develop theory comparable to that of modern science, the concern with empirical knowledge must be recaptured and accentuated if political theory was to be the "theoretical organ" of a contemporary science of politics.[8] In any event, he argued, historical studies must be demoted "to the more humble position of a useful device for nourishing the mind both with regard to creative values and causal theory."[9]

To a great extent, the study of the history of political theory came to be equated with the traditionalism that Easton and the other spokesmen for behavioralism attacked in their attempt to revolutionize political science and political theory. Some political scientists were more inclined than Easton to see a positive role for the history of political theory within the discipline of political science and suggested that it might yield interesting hypotheses for both explaining and recommending political behavior if it gave up the "Great Books" approach and its concern with the "history of ideas and historical biography."[10] They agreed with Easton that political science required a theoretical revolution, since it was the only social scientific discipline in which theory was identified with a study of the "philosophical literature of the past."[11] However, a history of political concepts could be justified to a limited extent if it produced propositions useful to scientific inquiry and public policy and if it complemented empirical investigations of political facts.

Although some political scientists continued to suggest a reconciliation between those who wished to appropriate the title of "political theory" for the intellectual core of a scientific study of politics and those who continued to equate "theory" with political evaluation and the history of political thought,[12] any resolution of the conflict remained largely conceptual. The discipline's official partition of political theory into empirical, normative, and historical sections during the 1960s reflected more the standard assumption that the practice of science required a strict separation of what is from what ought to be and the *de facto* situation of the study of political theory than any integrated approach to theorizing. Historians of political theory came to be the opposition party as the dominance of the behavioralists became more pronounced. They were also concerned with what they understood to be the decline of political theory, but in their view the decline was largely a function of modern political science's advocacy of scientific method and its neglect of what they believed to have been the traditional concerns of political theory.

Although Easton had ostensibly emphasized the need for a revival of political evaluation and the relationship between social scientific knowledge and political action, his principal concern, as well as that of most political scientists, was to distinguish discussions of values from descriptions and explanations of facts and to further the development of a purely empirical science of politics. Although Easton had warned of some of the practical dangers of value relativism and historicism, he accepted the basic premises of this analysis of values and the logical positivist's philosophical account of value judgments as primarily expressions of aesthetic or emotional preference that must be logically distinguished from empirical propositions. In response to the charge of irrelevance, historians of political theory such as Leo Strauss argued that the study of political thought of the past was of singular importance for a proper understanding of modern political phenomena as well as for the illumination and solution of contemporary political problems. They also charged that the attempt of modern political scientists to separate fact from value was an impossibility and a trivialization of political analysis rather than a new and progressive stage. Behavioralism, they insisted, was not a revival of the concerns of classic political philosophy but instead a false and truncated approach that neglected the wisdom of the past. It was itself a symptom of the decline of political theory. The issue was fast becoming a matter of who was the rightful heir to the Western tradition of a search for political knowledge.

In the same year that Easton published his critique of political science, Alfred Cobban asserted that the decline of the tradition and the malaise of contemporary political theory were products of theory's transformation into an academic discipline and its disengagement from the practical concerns that had animated Western political thought for twenty-five hundred years. He maintained that there was no great literature in political theory today, and that a tradition that had included Plato and Machiavelli might be coming to an end.[13] Although Cobban suggested that this loss of vision might be attributed in part to a growing pessimism about the influence of ethical values on political power, he argued that a principal cause was the domination of modes of thought associated with history and science. History, with its attachment to the past and its tendency toward relativistic thinking, and positivist science, with its disdain for evaluative claims and its dedication to a value-free approach to political analysis, had brought about an atrophication of creative political thinking.

During the 1950s there were numerous attempts to explain what generally was accepted as the demise of the long tradition of Western political theory and the disappearance of the literature that characterized this tradition.[14] I will consider some of these arguments in the following chapter, but, in many instances, the causes were in some way attributed to historicism and positivism, both of which tended to undercut the idea of rational claims regarding values. Commentators on both sides of the controversy generally assumed that an identifiable tradition of political theory was self-evident and was in a stage of decline, transition, or crisis. It was assumed also that the tradition was characterized by ethical or value judgments about politics and recommendations about the structure of political life. Consequently, the question of the contemporary state of the great tradition seemed closely tied to the general problem of the rational justification of values.

In the wake of positivist ethical theory and its account of the logic, or lack of logic, of moral judgment, philosophers such as T. D. Weldon argued, in effect, that the whole tradition of political theory rested on the mistaken belief that values could be objectively determined and rationally defended. According to Weldon, such judgments, unlike empirical judgments, lacked cognitive meaning and were matters of preference, ideology, or decision rather than matters for rational discussion.[15] In view of the growing influence of this position, Peter Laslett concluded in 1956 that the "tradition has been broken" and "political philosophy is dead."[16] Three years later, Arnold Brecht lamented the crisis in political theory that had resulted from the growing dominance of "scientific value relativism" and the conclusion that value claims could not be logically justified.[17]

By the 1960s, however, the literature of post-positivistic ethical philosophy had begun to have an impact on discussions of political theory. Positivist claims about the meaninglessness of evaluative language were beginning to give way before studies of the logic and language of morals that, while they tended to accept the positivist dichotomy between empirical and normative discourse, attempted to establish the autonomy and rationality of ethical argument. This philosophical development suggested to some that the epitaph for political theory had been premature. Just as the positivist analysis of ethics seemed to indicate the impossibility of political theory, the post-positivistic analysis of valuative judgment seemed to promise its possibility. As long as men debated social ends, the tradition of political theory would persist, and, with the renewed attention of philosophers to prescriptive discourse, it seemed safe to assume that "political philosophy in the English-speaking world is alive again" and "will not wholly perish from the earth."[18] There was a growing sense that the rescue of value judgments provided a basis for reviving the great tradition.

Since, according to most of the new work in ethical theory, factual reasons based on empirical data were essential to the justification of value judgments and, at the same time, all descriptions and explanations of facts inevitably took place within an evaluative framework, it seemed reasonable to assume that empirical and normative theory, and even social science and political philosophy, might be complementary. Political theory—factored into fact and value, the descriptive and the prescriptive, the empirical and the normative—seemed to many to have reestablished the scope of its original concerns and secured the tradition. Similarly, during the late 1960s and early 1970s in American political science, the idea of the mutually relevant character of normative and empirical theory has been widely accepted.[19]

With the emergence in the 1970s of what has been termed the "new revolution" in political science with its depreciation of "pure" social science in the short run in favor of public policy analysis and an applied social science relevant to an understanding and evaluation of practical issues,[20] the old debate about political theory seems to have subsided. Also, although the critique of political science by political theorists who study the history of political theory has not disappeared, the success of behavioralism in defining political science undermined the influence of this critique that to a large extent was directed at the very idea of a scientific study of politics. This dimension of the critique has largely given way to a variety of arguments that do not so much question the idea of a science of politics as they do the image of science characteristic of behavioralism's assumptions about the logic and the epistemology of empirical inquiry.[21] The history of political theory as a field of study remains associated with the discipline of political science, but by the 1970s historians of political theory, for the most part, had withdrawn to practice their own activity. However, part of the legacy of the debate about political theory was a confirmation of the tradition of political theory as distinct and worthy of study both as history and as the progenitor of modern political science.

When political theory is discussed primarily in functional

terms, such as making evaluative judgments about politics, the concept of a tradition and questions about its death and resurrection become abstract. However, there have been attempts to locate the reappearance of political theory more concretely in various contemporary philosophical positions such as existentialism, phenomenology, linguistic analysis, and post-Marxian critical theory that have addressed, or show promise of addressing, the political dimension of life.[22] Others have suggested that although political theory has suffered a decline, the death of political theory is a myth, and the "tradition of inquiry extending at least from Plato to Hegel" is enjoying a "revival" in the academic secondary literature on the history of political theory. Historians of political theory such as Leo Strauss, Eric Voegelin, and Hannah Arendt have, by analyzing the classic works in the great tradition in light of the modern age, revitalized that tradition.[23]

It is always possible to define political theory in a particular way, ascribe certain attributes to it, and then presume to discuss its past, present, and future. Most of the discussions from Easton onward have followed this mode of argument. Yet whether commentators proclaimed a degeneration of the tradition, condemned it as irrelevant to social science, perceived signs of its crisis, or forecast its revival, it was assumed that the classic texts from Plato to Marx were the components of a tradition that existed, or had existed, as a distinct historical entity. The idea of the tradition was a regulative paradigm in the study of politics as well as in the study of the history of political theory for many years. The idea of *the* tradition as an integral and evolving body of thought was most fully articulated in the course of these debates within political science about the relevance of the history of political theory, but it did not begin there.

Although Easton talked of a decline of the tradition and blamed it on historians who had lost sight of the real character of the activity that created that tradition, he was in fact referring to something that was largely an invention of the historians themselves. Easton's condemnation of research on the history of political theory badly misjudged, or misrepresented, what it had involved as well as the concerns of those who had practiced it.

THE HISTORY OF POLITICAL THEORY:
THE FORMATIVE YEARS

From a survey of studies in the history of political theory up through the early 1950s, two points which are important for understanding the subsequent developments in this field emerge quite clearly. First, these studies were seldom undertaken for merely academic reasons or motivated primarily by antiquarian concerns. They were conceived as directly relevant to contemporary problems and political values as well as to the development of an empirical political science usually viewed as having practical applications. Second, during this period, the assumptions that there was a distinct and major Western tradition of political theory comprised of the classic texts of political literature and that this tradition was the primary framework for interpreting particular works gained force. The "givenness" of the tradition became a basic scholarly convention.

In general, Easton was quite correct in noting that many of the historians whom he took to task were influenced by relativism, sociologism, historicism and similar positions which emphasized a close relationship between political ideas and their particular social and historical circumstances. This was largely the heritage of nineteenth century evolutionary social theory and philosophy of history that formed the intellectual context of most of the early studies in this field. However, although he also noted a tendency toward the use of "history to illuminate the meaning and to establish the worth of contemporary moral postulates,"[24] his characterization of this literature as principally providing an account of past ideas tended to belie the intentions of the authors and obscure the nature of their arguments. Specifically, Easton failed to note these individuals' deep concern with explaining and evaluating contemporary politics as well as with developing principles and concepts that would provide the foundation of a scientific, yet socially relevant, study of politics.

What is ironic is that the concerns of those engaged in writing the history of political theory were not significantly different from the concerns of Easton in his call for a new direction in political theory. What divided them principally were different conceptions of science and of the relevance of historical analysis. This, however, was hardly a new issue. In the early years of the development of political science as a distinct discipline in the United States there was little disagreement about the role of political theory in political science. Political theory was to supply the concepts necessary for the conduct of political science. The dispute was about the utility of the historical inductive method as opposed to notions of concept formation and causal explanation more closely related to those employed in sociology and psychology and about the derivation of concepts. Easton's critique of historicism closely resembled some of the attacks on historical-comparative method during the early 1900s. Political science's tendency to forget, or misinterpret, its own past and consequently to repeat that past is striking.[25]

From its earliest examples in the last half of the nineteenth century, what characterized the literature of the history of political theory was its sense of contributing to, and explaining, the development of political science and Western political values. Despite different conceptions of the precise relationship between politics and political ideas, as well as differences in substantive emphasis (for example, on law, political morality, or the state), the study of the evolution of political thought and institutions was viewed as basic to the search for universal political knowledge and the grounds of rational political action. As Robert Blakey said, in one of the first studies of the history of political literature, "political truth, like all other truth, expands and develops itself as time rolls." Historical studies explained the present by detailing "those various progressive steps or land-marks, in the great framework of European thought, on legislation and general government." The evolutionary perspective required a historical approach, and the emphasis was on political literature because it was believed to be the "direct and tangible expressions of politics."[26] To subsume these studies under the historicist model which Easton developed hardly serves accurately to characterize the concern with a science of politics or to indicate the extent to which this knowledge was considered relevant for political action. For some, the history of political ideas was viewed as a contribution to political education, and for nearly all it involved an attempt to trace the evolution of political science from the time of the Greeks and to discover the principles of political science that would provide knowledge of political phenomena and a basis for sound political decisions.[27]

Another influential writer of the late nineteenth century, Frederick Pollock, presented the history of political theory as the "history of the science of politics," and although he did not believe that such a science was yet equal to the exact or natural sciences, he saw one of its principal functions as that of critically exposing "wild speculation" and "absurd theories and projects."[28] It was clear from the beginning that the purpose of these studies was "not to revive the corpse of past erudition . . . but to make more vivid the life of today, and to help us envisage its problems with a more accurate perspective."[29]

William A. Dunning's influential three volume study, *A History of Political Theories* published between 1902 and 1920, did a great deal to establish this field of scholarship as a distinct discipline and to shape the basic concerns and assumptions that would dominate it for the next few decades. Dunning's work was the prototype of the genre that concentrated on tracing the development of the Western tradition of political thought through analysis of classic works and their historical context from Plato to the present. For individuals such as Dunning, research in the history of political theory and the practice of empirical political science were complementary efforts. The historical approach with its emphasis on facts was understood as an antidote to speculation, and the concern with political ideas was viewed as a deeper study of political phenomena that went beyond the static formalism of institutional analysis and captured the dynamic character of social activity. Many of the basic themes of this time would be repeated in later calls for a scientific study of politics, including those of the behavioral movement. Although there were considerable differences among scholars with regard to what constituted proper historical data, many argued that inductive history was a key to a science of politics and that the history of political theory was the heart of this enterprise. The emphasis on the historical method was already the concern of Dunning's teacher John W. Burgess, one of the founders of American political science, who saw such a science as a basis of citizen education. Before Dunning's work appeared, his own student, Charles E. Merriam, who later played such an important role in the development of political science and the idea of a scientific study of politics, had published a history of modern political theory which was clearly influenced by Dunning's approach.[30]

Dunning acknowledged his debt to earlier writers such as Pollock, but he believed that inadequate attention had been given to the history of political theories, which he described as the "successive transformations through which the political consciousness of men has passed."[31] Dunning believed that these transformations pointed toward a science of political society that would yield both contemplative and manipulative political knowledge, and he ended his long study with a consideration of the evolutionary philosophy of Herbert Spencer. He also praised the positivist sociology of Auguste Comte whose "work ranks with the greatest achievements of the human mind in generalizing from the past the elements of progress in civilization" and in specifying "the method and the utility of history."[32] Dunning argued that political theory consisted not only of political literature but of the operative ideas implicit in the legal institutions of the state and the political consciousness of a society. He believed that there was a "pretty definite and clearly discernible relationship between any given author's work and the current of institutional development," and he emphasized an "interpretation of the development of political theory in its relation to political fact."[33] This interpretation was largely devoted to demonstrating that modern political institutions and political science in the West were the culmination of an evolutionary process that began with the ancient Greeks.

For Dunning, political theory, as well as political consciousness, began with the Greeks, was largely limited to "the philosophy of the European Aryan peoples," and reflected the "progress" of the differentiation of political knowledge in the West.[34] He argued that the Greeks "explored the entire height and depth of human political capacity and outlined the principles which in all times and in all circumstances must determine the general features of political life" and that Greek thought on political authority contained "substantially all the solutions ever suggested."[35] For Dunning, the accomplishments of the Greeks in both science and politics were exemplary, and the study of the history of political theory demonstrated that in the course of the history of politics culminating in the present, the "movement of thought has but swung full circle." Yet at the same time, Dunning argued that, in its concrete expression, there has been, despite some gaps, evidence of progress in theory since the time of classical Greece. This was apparent, he suggested, in the transformation of views about slavery, the emergence of representative democracy, the appearance of a clear distinction between state and society, and the development of the modern concept of sovereignty.[36]

Some of the individuals, such as W. W. Willoughby, who were most influential in the discipline of political science during the early 1900s undertook studies in the history of political theory. Despite continuing debates about such matters as the relationship between political science and other disciplines (such as history, law, economics, and sociology) and between political science and practical politics, nearly everyone agreed that the role of political theory was to develop the concepts and principles of a scientific political science and that the history of political theory was a central part of this project. Willoughby argued that political theories were closely related to political fact. They were not only "dependent upon" and "evoked by . . . objective conditions" but reflected the "actuating motives" of political action and therefore were important in explaining political events. He believed that historical studies were important for scientific understanding and that the historical method required no defense.[37] He distinguished his study from Dunning's on the basis that he gave more attention to the "political presuppositions" embedded in the "objective facts" rather than merely looking at the literature of political theory.[38] However, they both stressed the various ways in which political theories and political facts were related and were mutually explanatory. Along with Merriam, many came to reject the historical method and to see political science in the 1920s as moving into a new stage of empirical science emphasizing quantitative techniques and approaches closely identified with sociology and psychology. Nevertheless, they did not oppose their work to the history of political theory and particularly not to the concerns that had informed it. The rejection of the historical method was not equivalent to a rejection of the history of political theory as irrelevant to the discipline of political science. In fact, Merriam's approach to political analysis was in many respects closely related to Dunning's concern with the relationship between political ideas and their social ambience.[39] Further, to a great extent the history of political theory was viewed as the history of political science.

In 1924, Raymond G. Gettell, whose popular textbook in political science had been published in 1910, attempted in much the same manner as Dunning to trace the "development of political thought in relation to its historical, institutional, and intellectual background."[40] It is worth noting that for individuals such as Gettell the belief that political ideas do not embody absolute and demonstrable truths but are relative to historical circumstances was not at all in conflict with the belief that in both ideas and institutions there was a movement toward democracy.[41] For Gettell, the writing of the history of political theory produced scholarship of intrinsic worth apart from any practical application, but he stressed its contribution to clarity and precision in political thought and its relevance to contemporary politics as a basis for rational action in democratic society.[42] It generally was accepted that the "theory of politics is the peculiar product of Western thought" and that there was not "a single controversy of our day without a pedigree stretching into the distant ages."[43]

Similar themes are apparent in the work of C. H. McIllwain who was one of Easton's principal targets of criticism. In his treatise on the *Growth of Political Thought in the West*, he noted the close tie between political ideas and institutions, and he stressed that the history of political theory serves to illuminate "the *development* of our ideas about the state and about government" and the "*growth*" of thought about the basic problems of political obligation. This was an "evolutionary process" that began in ancient Greece where "we find the first faint trickle of that particular stream" of ideas that has been central to European culture. According to McIlwain, this organic development culminated in the theory and practice of modern "*legislative* sovereignty."[44]

During the 1930s, the literature on the history of political theory crystalized as a distinct and popular genre. The motivation behind the proliferation of surveys of the history of political theory in the 1930s and 1940s was in part a concern with exploring the background of the twentieth century confrontation between Western liberalism and totalitarian ideologies and justifying democratic institutions and values. This emphasis on understanding "the contemporary struggle between totalitarianism . . . and constitutionalism," and tracing the evolution of "constitutional democracy," continued into the post–World War II period.[45] However, by 1930 the idea that there was a tradition of political theory that was relevant for understanding contemporary politics and that had evolved continuously from the time of ancient Greece to become sufficiently well-defined to be a standard subject of college textbooks and academic research in political science was accepted. "To study the history of political ideas is to study our own ideas and see how we came to hold them."[46] Again, it should be stressed that at this point the continuing debate in political science about historical methods had little to do with the history of political theory. Certainly, apart from Merriam, no one was more concerned with defending the idea of a scientific study of politics than George Catlin. Catlin denied that history, which deals with particulars, could be the basis of a general science of politics, and he rejected the notion, characteristic of some of the earlier work in the history of political theory, that historical analysis could be the source of basic concepts in political science or provide general knowledge of politics and laws of political development.[47] Nevertheless, Catlin was the author of one of the several histories of political theory that appeared in the 1930s.

Like many of the writers of this period, Catlin was concerned with what he believed to be the political effects of the dogmas of Hegelianism, Marxism, and fascism. He believed, like the scholars who preceded him, that his study had revealed a "rational Grand Tradition of Culture and also (quite distinct) the beginnings of a Science of Politics" and that it was possible to "mount upon the bastion of three thousand years a searchlight that may project forward a ray for a few decades toward the horizon of the human future."[48] Like previous writers, Catlin acknowledged that political ideas are reflections of time and place and yet maintained that he could find progress and meaning in their development. It was also clear that Catlin believed that the tradition of political ideas itself was in part the source of contemporary political problems and that there were very practical reasons for undertaking a history of political ideas. He was either more self-conscious or candid than many when he announced that although his work "wears the fleece of a history of political philosophy, it is but fair that I should warn the reader that it is written as a philosophy of political history."[49] In this respect, Catlin's approach was an indication of the direction that the history of political theory would take after 1950.

Easton correctly noted that Sabine's *A History of Political Theory,* first published in 1937, had "exercised deeper influence over the study of political theory in the United States during recent years than any other single work."[50] This book became an essential element in the education of graduate as well as undergraduate students and provided the basic model for numerous textbooks as well as particular scholarly studies. To understand Sabine is to understand a good deal about this field, but Easton's analysis, which is largely a statement about Sabine's failure to reconstruct moral values and political goals, does not go very far toward such an understanding. More than anything else, Sabine's work established the idea of the tradition of political theory as a given and lent authority to the assumption that it had been a determinative influence on contemporary modes of political thought and action. In its successive editions, Sabine's text became more and more an explicit affirmation of the idea that "political theory is an intellectual tradition and its history consists of the evolution of men's thoughts about political problems over time."[51] The tradition did not consist of merely " 'any thinking about politics or relevant to politics' " but was "a collection of writings" that had been primarily the product of "philosophical writers" and their " 'disciplined' investigation of political problems and as such it was invented at a particular place, namely among the Hellenes in what we now call Greece, and at a more or less specific time, during the fifth century before Christ."[52] For Sabine, the tradition of political theory was not merely an analytical construct but a concrete historical phenomenon which, despite its apparent diversity, had been "a unit throughout its history."[53] In Sabine's view, these works constituted a natural unit in that they possessed numerous similarities such as their emergence in times of crisis, but he also strengthened the assumption that they were largely the product of a recognizable activity which could be traced historically and that the history of Western political thought could be viewed in a holistic manner.

The importance of these works, according to Sabine, was not merely that they had been produced as a "normal part of the social *milieu* in which politics itself has its being," and therefore disclosed something about the past, but that they had been an "intrinsic element of the whole political process" and thus contributed to our knowledge of the present.[54] To suggest, as Easton does, that in Sabine's work "the study of theory is reduced to historical narration" with no clear idea of its relevance to contemporary values is misleading.[55] Sabine identified his position as "social relativism," on the assumption that to understand a theory requires that it be located in the context of particular political circumstances and viewed as a reaction to certain political facts.[56] Yet his history was intended as a critical, interpretative work which presented an overall picture of the evolution of political ideas in such a way as to justify certain political doctrines and demonstrate the limitations of others. As in some earlier writings on the subject, there was a definite sense of progression toward Western democracy and pluralism despite the aberrations of totalitarian ideologies. Sabine made it clear that those ideas which have survived are the fittest and that they not only gave an accurate analysis of their contemporary situation but were relevant to the more perennial problems of politics and thus often became part of the world of politics itself.

Sabine argued, as did many political scientists of this period as well as later advocates of scientific political inquiry such as Easton, that political theory usually consists of three kinds of logically distinct propositions: factual, causal, and evaluative. Since theories often are comprised mostly of evaluative elements that, in Sabine's view (following Hume), were not derivable from facts or demonstrable in terms of facts, he suggested that, as a whole, a theory "can hardly be said to be true."[57] However, its influence and utility can be assessed, and he believed that (by identifying and discriminating between the various kinds of propositions in a theory, examining its internal consistency, and judging the validity of its causal and empirical claims) critical analysis was possible. For Sabine, some theories involved a systematic conflation of fact and value, and the defect, for example, of Hegel's arguments—as well as other political theory which had been influenced by his work, including to some degree modern pragmatism—was the fallacy that logic, fact, and value could be synthesized. In many respects, Sabine's argument was quite compatible with the claims of individuals such as Catlin who distinguished between political theory as part of a political science and political theory as political philosophy or aesthetically grounded value judgments.[58] The mistake of Marxism, according to Sabine, was its claim to a kind of scientific knowledge that lay outside the realm of empirical verification. Like his predecessors, Sabine was wary of the political consequences of speculative thought and, like many political scientists, saw an ameliorative tendency in what he believed were the mutually supportive developments of scientific thinking and democracy.

For the most part, it is difficult to discern in this literature, up through the late 1940s, the source of Easton's portrayal of either the character of scholarship in the history of political theory or the intentions and concerns that gave rise to it. Despite their historical orientation, these authors were concerned with both contemporary values and the advancement of a scientific study of politics. They were certainly not involved in studying the past for its own sake. It would be a mistake to suggest that behavioralism did not introduce innovation into the discipline of political science, but it would also be a mistake to assume that it constituted a radical change in the general goals and distribution of emphasis that had characterized American political science during most of the twentieth century. In many respects, the continuities were as important as the transformations, and although behavioralism may have rejected a study of the history of political ideas and institutions as essential to its project, and even designated it as an obstacle to scientific progress, the history of political theory remained a subfield of political science and carried with it the legacy of a belief in the reality of the great tradition as both the past of modern political science and the source of modern political values.

POLITICAL THEORY
AND THE HISTORY OF IDEAS

In recent years the tension between historians of political theory and defenders of contemporary trends in political science has abated. There are still those who speak the language of the debate between an old and new political science, but it is of diminishing consequence for both research and teaching. As I suggested earlier, this has been less the result of an intellectual rapprochement or a recognition of complementarity than the product of continuing disciplinary differentiation. Although there are still discussions of the relevance of the classics to contemporary political science,[59] any close relationship between the study of the history of political theory and the conduct of inquiry in political science is not at all apparent. To some extent, this increased intellectual distance may account for a certain turning inward on the part of historians of political theory and a growing concern with the nature of their enterprise. They are concerned with justifying it on its own terms rather than as a remedy for the deficiencies of political science. There has been an increase in reflection about methodological problems of the interpretation of the classical texts that have characteristically constituted the subject matter of this field, and important philosophical issues about understanding and explanation have been raised that are, in many respects, common to most of the humanities and social sciences.[60] Once these problems have been broached, it is not easy to be complacent about the general character, as well as the specific claims, of much of the most influential scholarship in this field. Yet any critical examination of past scholarship, as well as proposals for alternative modes of inquiry, requires a clear grasp of the types of concerns which have motivated it.

It has been suggested that within the last decade there has been a "transformation" which signals "the emergence of a truly autonomous method" for studying the history of political theory.[61] Any such transformation is not yet generally evident, but it would be fair to say that a new level of critical awareness has been generated. The principal thesis of much of the literature that announces, or calls for, a different approach is that past research has not been adequately historical and has suffered, because of its methodological deficiencies, from an inability to recover the actual meaning of texts and satisfactorily describe and explain persistence and change in political ideas. The critics argue that research has been dominated by various types of preconceptions, both procedural and substantive, which have distorted interpretations of writings from the past and explanations of the development of ideas.[62] There is no doubt that a serious and important challenge to some of the prevailing assumptions in the field is emerging, and I will return to this issue in Chapter IV. Yet despite the importance of the problems that have been raised regarding the infirmities of past research, and notwithstanding the possible merits of some of the positive arguments about historical interpretation, there has been a tendency for the critics to violate one of their own methodological prescriptions. This is the need to attend to the actual intentions of an author and the particular intellectual context of his argument in order to adequately understand the meaning of his work. Recent criticism of the historical integrity of much of the literature on the history of political theory has, like the earlier criticism, often failed to appreciate its actual character. It is somewhat ironic that it was its alleged failure as a practical enterprise and its supposed emphasis on historical narration that brought it under attack by individuals such as Easton, while it is now a charge of lacking historicity which forms the basis of the contemporary critique.

The critics often approach the secondary literature in the history of political theory as if it were a subfield of the history of ideas which could be distinguished and identified in terms of its particular subject matter, that is, political ideas. There is also an assumption that the history of ideas may be treated as if it were a specific activity or discipline and, consequently, that it is possible and valid both to discuss methodological problems in the history of ideas in terms of various examples from scholarship in the history of political theory and to view research in the history of political theory in terms of concerns and purposes attributed to the history of ideas. However, it is doubtful that it is reasonable to assume that the history of ideas refers to a distinct activity with any common disciplinary matrix and research program or that it is anything more than a generic category for work in a number of fields that bear certain family resemblances (history of religion, history of science, history of philosophy, etc.). In addition, it is a mistake to presume that the various types of literature that may be classed within the history of ideas have the same degree of coherence. While the history of science, for example, may, despite certain sharp methodological controversies, constitute a relatively well-defined field of study, the history of political theory is not a comparable discipline. Although it is recognized as a subfield of political science, its practitioners are by no means always political scientists, and it is far from immediately apparent that all the literature that is usually considered as belonging to this field belongs to a distinct genre. There are good reasons for suggesting that, like the history of ideas, the history of political theory is a category that encompasses a quite diverse body of literature rather than a designation for a clearly circumscribed activity with generally accepted standards of judgment and procedures of analysis.

It may be true that much of the research in the history of political theory has lacked any definite criteria for evaluating the adequacy of arguments regarding both interpretations of the meaning of texts and explanations of the development of political ideas. Yet, prior to any critical analysis of such research, it is necessary to clarify precisely what literature is involved and to approach this analysis as an examination of the kind of enterprise in which particular historians are engaged. It is not adequate simply to assume that this literature is intelligible as a species of the history of ideas which can, in turn, be viewed as an antiseptic search for the historical meaning of classic texts. One might argue that this is what scholars should be doing, but it is necessary to determine first what in fact they are, and have been, doing. What, from one perspective, may seem to be deficiencies in historical method may appear somewhat differently if the aim was not in fact historical.

Any careful review of the most influential commentaries on the history of political theory would reveal a profound concern with the present condition of political theory and the implications for both politics and the study of politics. Since any understanding of the present in terms of the past is taken as crucial, the problem of how properly and authoritatively to acquire historical knowledge is seldom severed from the problem of why such knowledge is necessary. Yet, the prevailing perspective has often been what Michael Oakeshott terms a practical rather than a historical attitude toward the past.[63] These categories are not free from difficulty as a basis for characterizing arguments about the past, yet if taken as a way of sorting activities, rather than evaluating claims to knowledge and determining what is a valid historical argument, they do serve to discriminate certain important differences in concern, approach, and distribution of emphasis.

While the historical attitude shows a tendency to treat the past as an object intrinsically worthy of investigation, the practical attitude shows a concern with the past in relation to the present. Although Oakeshott emphasizes the contemplative or disinterested posture of the historian, the difference is not simply one of objectivity or the absence of an ideological framework and other kinds of regulative assumptions. While the historical attitude is concerned with producing a concrete account of the past, the practical attitude tends to approach the past in terms derived from the present, to read events backward and make sense of the past in relation to the present, to select what is relevant for discussing contemporary problems, and to justify and condemn.

Although in many respects the various commentaries on the history of political theory may be too diverse to allow a general characterization, much of the literature that has been most important in defining the content of the field and the approaches to inquiry in recent years, as well as before the 1950s, has been distinguished by a practical attitude. Whether or not the field is now undergoing a transformation and casting off its practical concerns in favor of a more historical orientation, past scholarship cannot be examined critically under the assumption that its practitioners had the same view of their enterprise as the critics.

As I indicated previously, the response of historians of political theory to the challenge by behavioralists regarding the importance of studying the tradition was not merely to reaffirm that it was relevant for both political science and politics but to maintain that it was now absolutely crucial. Historical reflection on the tradition was important, in a sense that went far beyond the assumptions of earlier scholars, for an understanding and solution of what they announced as the fundamental crisis of political thought and action in the modern age. The developments of contemporary political science, they maintained, were not salutary innovations but rather intellectual tendencies that were both symptoms and causes of a decline of the tradition and representative of the fate of political thought. The critique of the history of political theory was countered with an attack on political science as the culmination of a rejection of traditional knowledge that began with modern political theory and was fast creating a crisis in existential politics. Historians of political theory came to represent themselves as the last outpost of an old political science and as the remnant of the tradition itself. What came to distinguish much of the most influential literature on the history of political theory after 1950 was a concern with the pathology of the tradition, rather than its progress, and a critical attitude toward the philosophical foundations of contemporary politics, political thought, and political science.

Although the assumption of the reality of the tradition as an inherited pattern of thought steadily matured during the twentieth century, the acceptance of this assumption became absolutely pivotal in the 1950s and 1960s in the arguments of many of the principal historians of political theory which depended on a substantive vision of the development and impact of the tradition. In the very early literature, the notion of a tradition, linking as it did only apparently similar kinds of political literature, was vague. Under the influence of various theories of cultural evolution and progress, individuals such as Dunning began to treat this material more as an organic intellectual unit. As the search for the roots of Marxism and fascism and the defense of democracy became important, the idea of a coherent tradition with causative implications for the present became more prevalent. Finally, as historians of political theory found themselves forced to justify their endeavor in the face of attacks from modern social science, the notion of a tradition that not only explained the present but demonstrated the deficiencies of the modern study of politics and, at least in some measure, promised a solution to contemporary problems, became a persistent element in this literature. Although different ideas about the content and meaning of the tradition would emerge, the idea of the tradition developed into a paradigmatic assumption in teaching and research in this field.

NOTES

1. David Easton, "The Decline of Modern Political Theory," *Journal of Politics* 13 (February 1951): 36–37.

2. Ibid., pp. 40, 43.

3. David Easton, *The Political System: An Inquiry into the State of Political Science* (New York: Knopf, 1953), p. 254.

4. Easton, "The Decline of Modern Political Theory," p. 41.

5. Easton, *The Political System,* p. 233.

6. Ibid., p. 234.

7. Easton, "The Decline of Modern Political Theory," p. 38.

8. Ibid., pp. 51–52.

9. Ibid., p. 58.

10. See Andrew Hacker, "Capital and Carbuncles: The 'Great Books' Reappraised," *American Political Science Review* 48 (September 1954): 755–86.

11. See William A. Glaser, "The Types and Uses of Political Theory," *Social Research* 22 (October 1955): 275–96.

12. See Harry Eckstein, "The Condition and Prospect of Political Thought," *American Political Science Review* 50 (June 1956): 475–87.

13. Alfred Cobban, "Ethics and the Decline of Political Theory," *Political Science Quarterly* 68 (September 1953): 322.

14. See, for example, Judith Sklar, *After Utopia* (Princeton: Princeton University Press, 1957).

15. See T. D. Weldon, *The Vocabulary of Politics* (London: Penguin, 1953) and "Political Principles," in Peter Laslett, ed., *Philosophy, Politics and Society,* First Series (Oxford: Blackwell, 1956).

16. Laslett, *Philosophy, Politics and Society*, pp. vii, ix.

17. Arnold Brecht, *Political Theory: The Foundations of Twentieth Century Political Thought* (Princeton: Princeton University Press, 1959).

18. Peter Laslett, "Introduction," in Peter Laslett and W. G. Runciman, eds., *Philosophy, Politics and Society*, Third Series (New York: Barnes and Noble, 1967), p. 3; Isaiah Berlin, "Does Political Theory Still Exist?" in Peter Laslett and W. G. Runciman, eds., *Philosophy, Politics and Society*, Second Series (New York: Barnes and Noble, 1962), p. 33.

19. For a discussion of these issues, see John G. Gunnell, *Philosophy, Science, and Political Inquiry* (Morristown, N.J.: General Learning Press, 1975), Chs. 7, 8.

20. See David Easton, "The New Revolution in Political Science," *American Political Science Review* 63 (December 1969).

21. See Gunnell, *Philosophy, Science, and Political Inquiry*, Chs. 1–6.

22. See, for example, Richard J. Bernstein, *The Restructuring of Social and Political Theory* (New York: Harcourt, Brace & Jovanovich, 1976).

23. Dante Germino, *Beyond Ideology: The Revival of Political Theory* (New York: Harper, 1967), pp. 2, 17.

24. Easton, *The Political System*, p. 257.

25. For discussions of the history of political science, see Bernard Crick, *The American Science of Politics: Its Origins and Conditions* (Berkeley: University of California Press, 1959); Anna Haddow, *Political Science in American Colleges and Universities* (New York: Appleton-Century, 1939); Albert Somit and Joseph Tanenhaus, *The Development of American Political Science: From Burgess to Behavioralism* (Boston: Allyn and Bacon, 1967). While the Crick and Somit and Tanenhaus volumes tend toward polemics and apologetics, respectively, a more balanced overview is presented by Dwight Waldo, "Political Science: Tradition, Discipline, Profession, Science, Enterprise," in Fred I. Greenstein and Nelson W. Polsby, eds., *Handbook of Political Science*, vol. 1, *Political Science: Scope and Theory* (Reading: Addison-Wesley, 1975).

26. Robert Blakey, *The History of Political Literature* (London: Richard Bentley, 1855), pp. i, vi.

27. Ibid., p. xii.

28. Frederick Pollock, *An Introduction to the History of the Science of Politics* (London: Macmillan, 1890), pp. 1, 4.

29. John Neville Figgis, *Studies of Political Thought from Gerson to Grotius, 1414–1625* (Cambridge: Cambridge University Press, 1907), p. 3.

30. Charles E. Merriam, *History of the Theory of Sovereignty Since Rousseau* (New York: Columbia University, 1900).

31. William A. Dunning, *A History of Political Theories, Ancient and Medieval* (New York: Macmillan, 1902), p. viii. The second volume of Dunning's work was *A History of Political Theories, From Luther to Montesquieu* (New York: Macmillan, 1905).

32. William A. Dunning, *A History of Political Theories, From Rousseau to Spencer* (New York: Macmillan, 1920), p. 393.

33. Dunning, *Ancient and Medieval*, pp. xviii–xix, xxv.

34. Ibid., p. xix.

35. Ibid., p. 1; Dunning, *From Rousseau to Spencer*, p. 416.

36. Dunning, *From Rousseau to Spencer*, pp. 423, 410.

37. Westel Woodbury Willoughby, *The Political Theories of the Ancient World* (New York: Longmans, Green, 1903), pp. v, vii.

38. Ibid., p. xii.

39. See Charles E. Merriam, ed., *A History of Political Theories, Recent Times* (New York: Macmillan, 1924); Merriam, *New Aspects of Politics* (Chicago: Chicago University Press, 1925).

40. Raymond G. Gettell, *History of Political Thought* (New York: Century, 1924), p. v.

41. Ibid., pp. 5, 6, 16, 17.

42. Ibid., pp. 17–19.

43. A. R. Lord, *The Principles of Politics* (London: Oxford University Press, 1921), p. 11; Robert H. Murray, *The History of Political Science from Plato to the Present* (New York: D. Appleton, 1925), preface.

44. Charles Howard McIlwain, *The Growth of Political Thought in the West* (New York: Macmillan, 1932), pp. v, 3, 201, 390–92.

45. William Y. Elliot and Neil A. McDonald, *Western Political Heritage* (New York: Prentice-Hall, 1949), p. vii. See, for example, John Bowle, *Western Political Thought* (London: Jonathan Cape, 1947); Phyllis Doyle, *A History of Political Thought* (London: Jonathan Cape, 1933); Chester C. Maxey, *Political Philosophies* (New York: Macmillan, 1938).

46. Thomas I. Cook, *History of Political Philosophy from Plato to Burke* (New York: Prentice-Hall, 1936), p. 13; Francis W. Coker, *Readings in Political Philosophy* (New York: Macmillan, 1938), p. vii and *Recent Political Thought* (New York: D. Appleton-Century, 1934), p. 1; R. H. S. Crossman, *Government and the Governed* (London: Christophers, 1939), p. 5.

47. Cf. Gaetano Mosca, *A Short History of Political Philosophy*, trans. Sondra Z. Koff (New York: Thomas Y. Crowell, 1972).

48. George Catlin, *The Story of the Political Philosophers* (New York: McGraw-Hill, 1939), p. x.

49. Ibid.

50. Easton, *The Political System,* p. 249.

51. George H. Sabine, *A History of Political Theory,* 4th ed., rev. Thomas Landon Thorson (Hinsdale, Ill.: Dryden Press, 1973), p. 3.

52. Ibid., p. 4.

53. George H. Sabine, "What is a Political Theory?" *Journal of Politics* I (February 1939): 2.

54. George H. Sabine, *A History of Political Theory* (New York: Holt, Rinehart, and Winston, 1938), p. v.

55. Easton, *The Political System,* p. 251.

56. Sabine, *A History of Political Theory,* p. vi.

57. Ibid., p. vi; "What is a Political Theory," pp. 1–16.

58. George E. G. Catlin, "Political Theory: What Is It?" *Political Science Quarterly* 77 (March 1957): 1–29.

59. Dante Germino, "The Contemporary Relevance of the Classics of Political Philosophy," in Greenstein and Polsby, *Political Science,* pp. 229–281.

60. See Quentin Skinner, "Meaning and Understanding in the History of Ideas," *History and Theory* 8 (1969): 3–53 and "Some Problems in the Analysis of Political Thought and Action," *Political Theory* 2 (August 1974): 277–303. For critical discussions of Skinner's arguments and further analysis of these problems, see Richard Ashcraft, "On the Problem of Methodology and the Nature of Political Theory," *Political Theory* 3 (February 1975): 5–25; Bhiku Parekh and R. N. Berki, "The History of Political Ideas: A Critique of Q. Skinner's Methodology," *Journal of History of Ideas* 34 (1973): 163–84; Margaret Leslie, "In Defense of Anachronism," *Political Studies* 4 (1970): 433–47; J. G. A. Pocock, *Politics, Language, and Time* (New York: Atheneum, 1971); Gordon Schochet, "Quentin Skinner's Method," *Political Theory* 2 (August 1974): 261–76; Charles Tarlton, "Historicity, Meaning and Revisionism in the Study of Political Thought," *History and Theory* 12 (1973): 307–28.

61. Pocock, *Politics, Language, and Time,* p. 11.

62. See Skinner, "Meaning and Understanding in the History of Ideas."

63. Michael Oakeshott, *Rationalism in Politics* (London: Methuen, 1962), pp. 137–67.

Jean Jacques Rousseau 1712–1778

II

The Idea of the Tradition and the Crisis of Political Theory

Our tradition of political thought had its definite beginnings in the teachings of Plato and Aristotle. I believe it came to a no less definite end in the theories of Karl Marx.

Arendt

INTRODUCTION

The belief that one could speak of *the* tradition as the subject of commentaries and courses on the history of political theory was most fully expressed in arguments that sought to justify a continuing scholarly concern with what had come to be accepted as the classic texts of political literature. These arguments employed the idea of the tradition as a vehicle for a critique of contemporary political thought and action, including contemporary political science. By the 1940s, the notion that the tradition was in some sense an organic whole with a discernible form and meaning (usually the development of constitutional democracy) had gained prominence, but it was during the 1950s and 1960s that the assumptions characteristic of the idea of the tradition developed a firm hold on the history of political theory as a field of study. Most important is the assumption that the conventional chronology of classic works (including at least those of Plato, Aristotle, St. Augustine, St. Thomas Aquinas, Machiavelli, Hobbes, Locke, Rousseau, and Marx) is the product of a distinct activity and constitutes a definite tradition of inquiry extending well over two millennia. However, what had formerly been perceived as a process of evolution has come to be understood as one of devolution. It is generally accepted that this tradition began in Greece with Socrates and Plato but that in the modern age it has died, declined, or in some manner reached a crisis that corresponds to, and in some respect is related to, a general "crisis in Western civilization."[1]

Although the principal source of the modern crisis is usually located in the past, contemporary political and social scientific inquiry is viewed as both a symptom of a decadent tradition and a principal intellectual force that must be confronted. Yet the problem is not considered to be merely intellectual in nature, since it is assumed that the decline of the tradition has been responsible, in some very fundamental sense, for the debased condition of modern politics. Consequently, to engage in the interpretation of the history of political theory is far from a merely academic exercise. It is an explicitly therapeutic undertaking designed to diagnose modern ills, illuminate their origin and suggest, at least in general terms, the basis for a restoration of political health.

It is a *recherche de temps perdu* that seeks to probe the political psyche of the West and isolate that point, or points, when its derangement began. Usually it is argued that the tradition developed to a certain stage of knowledge but then degenerated or was fundamentally diverted. The specification of this critical juncture is a matter of particular importance. At the same time, it is usually assumed that a study of the tradition will reveal a counterpart to this intellectual detour, that is, a moment, or moments, of truth or enlightenment that can be recaptured by retracing the course of the tradition from the point of its contemporary crisis. As severe as this crisis may be, however, it is also viewed as felicitous in that it breaks the spell of the tradition and frees thought for a reflective and critical study of the past for the sake of the present. It is at once destructive and reconstructive; it is a cathartic venture in the discovery of error and the recovery of truth. Seldom is it suggested that this knowledge of the past and from the past can immediately provide a political recipe for the present, but it is assumed that it supplies a fundamental grasp of the nature of political phenomena that must be the starting point for any attempt to restructure modern political thought and action.

Once this basic conceptual scheme is accepted, there arise substantive questions about the meaning of the tradition as a whole, its import for the present, and the meaning and place of specific works within the tradition. There are also problems about the method for extracting this meaning and the criteria for judging particular interpretations. These questions occasion debates among historians and schools of interpretation, but, as important as the issues in these debates may be to the participants, they seldom touch the common premises that support the idea of the tradition and provide the unarticulated framework of these discussions.

Only a few scholars have actively elaborated substantive accounts of the tradition, and probably many historians of political theory would suscribe neither to any particular account nor to all the assumptions that are common to these various versions. Nevertheless, most commentaries on the history of political theory, whether overall interpretations of the tradition, textbook surveys, or analyses of specific classic works, have been deeply affected by the idea of the tradition and have contributed, at least tacitly, to its perpetuation. The idea of the tradition has become a paradigm for research and teaching, and to understand this field of study, it is necessary to understand the general features of this paradigm.

Certain writers have been particularly influential in defining and propagating this paradigm. By discussing the arguments of Leo Strauss, Eric Voegelin, Hannah Arendt, and Sheldon Wolin and their accounts of the decline of the tradition, I do not intend to imply that they speak authoritatively for the whole field. I am, however, suggesting that they have significantly contributed to the widespread entrenchment of the idea of the tradition in the secondary literature of the history of political theory and have had a profound impact on both teaching and research.

LEO STRAUSS: THE REJECTION
OF CLASSICAL POLITICAL PHILOSOPHY

Strauss is explicit that his research in the history of political philosophy is not the result of antiquarian concerns or merely scholarly interest in recovering the meaning of classical texts.[2] He also distinguishes his work from those historicist interpretations which either view political philosophy as a reflection of a particular historical situation or selectively reinterpret the past from the perspective of the present.[3] Yet for Strauss the study of the past is very much a practical matter. The attempt to understand the works of past political philosophers and the course of the development of political ideas within the Western tradition is required by what he diagnoses as "the crisis of our time, the crisis of the West."[4] the goal is to separate error from truth and restore past knowledge of political phenomena, especially knowledge concerning the nature of the good political society, which has been forgotten or obscured.

The crisis that Strauss alleges, the decline of the West and the imminence of tyranny, is a result of the external threat of communist totalitarianism and the internal degeneration of liberal democracy into a permissive moral relativism which, in its rejection of all absolutes, is incapable of defending its own principles. However, the political crisis is the result of a more fundamental intellectual crisis that is characterized by the decline of political philosophy.[5] Thus an understanding of that decline is a prerequisite for illuminating and solving the modern crisis, and an understanding of the decline in turn requires a penetration of the tradition within which political philosophy originally appeared and finally all but disappeared.

Strauss defines political philosophy as an activity that seeks "to replace opinion about the nature of political things by knowledge of the nature of political things" and, particularly, knowledge of the right political order.[6] He maintains that political philosophy was begun by Socrates, developed fully by Plato and Aristotle, and continued, at least in an attenuated form, until the present when it fell into "a state of decay and perhaps of putrefaction, if it has not vanished altogether."[7] The immediate cause of the demise of political philosophy was the emergence in the modern age of positivism and historicism which, by denying objective knowledge of values and asserting the relativity of all values, have destroyed the intellectual foundations of the activity.[8] With the decline of political philosophy has come the rise of social science with its tendencies toward historicism and positivism. Contemporary political science is at once the heir to the tradition of political philosophy and the manifestation of its fate in the modern age. Positivism and historicism have led to relativism and finally to nihilism, or the refusal to recognize the precedence of any one value over another, and although contemporary social science "fosters not so much nihilism as conformism and philistinism," it is closely tied to the intellectual and political crisis of the West.[9] Strauss argues that the new science of politics, characterized by the scientism of American political science and its claims of freedom from evaluative judgments, functions as an educational institution that supports relativistic liberalism. By blurring the doctrinal distinction between democracy and communism and treating them as merely different and incommensurable ideologies, it refuses to recognize tyranny for "what it really is."[10]

Since, for Strauss, the modern crisis is a direct consequence of the decline of political philosophy, historical studies are required in order to trace the origin and course of that decline.[11] He insists, however, that political philosophy itself, unlike the study of the history of political philosophy, is not a historical discipline, since it seeks transhistorical truths about politics.[12] Although the transformation of political philosophy into the history of political philosophy is the result of historicism, the study of the history of political philosophy is demanded by the particular circumstances of our time in order to seek out the roots of the Western crisis and to restore political philosophy and the knowledge that was once acquired by past political philosophy but is now lost or distorted. At the present moment of crisis and the final collapse of the tradition, it becomes possible to break free of the tradition and undertake an objective and self-conscious account of its development for the purpose of dealing with contemporary problems. Only now is it possible to scrutinize the assumptions of modernity that are the legacy of the tradition and "to understand in an untraditional and fresh manner what was hitherto only understood in a traditional or derivative manner."[13] At this point, it becomes possible to "understand the thinkers of the past exactly as they understood themselves" and to subject past thought to a critical examination which will separate truth from falsehood.[14]

Strauss maintains that classical political philosophy is the true science of politics and that a universal knowledge of politics is embodied in the work of Aristotle.[15] Here *"the* true political philosophy" appeared, and *"the* political truth" was discovered.[16] Classical political philosophy emerged with the origins of politics in the Greek polis and at a moment of crisis in that culture which, like the crisis of the contemporary age, forced the philosopher to seek the nature of political phenomena and the character of the best political order. Yet this was not a historical search, since, unlike the contemporary philosopher who must engage in historical studies and employ historical techniques, the classical philosopher apprehended politics "with a freshness and directness which never have been equalled." This original perception was untainted by the accretions of the tradition; all later understanding of politics has necessarily been derivative and mediated by tradition-laden concepts that stand between the philosopher and political phenomena.[17]

While the concepts of classical political philosophy were original and explicable in terms of political phenomena themselves, our concepts are secondary or traditional, and their true meaning can be understood only by historical study. To understand political things today, standing as we do at the end of the tradition, requires a historical detour that will regain the original vision achieved by classical political philosophy. Yet this, in turn, requires an analysis of the beginning of modern political philosophy which was based on a conscious rejection of the classical teaching and which can be understood accurately only in contrast with classical political philosophy. Strauss argues that if we are to restore classical knowledge, it is necessary to reopen that old quarrel between the ancients and moderns which precipitated the decline of political philosophy and eventually culminated in the modern crisis.[18] The history of political philosophy is the history of the progressive deterioration of the tradition and the contamination of classical knowledge, but the crucial division is between the classical and modern periods.

Strauss maintains that just as Socrates was the founder of classical political philosophy, Machiavelli was "the founder of modern political philosophy" and the originator of the premises that have come to inform all modern political thought from Karl Marx to contemporary political science, as well as the theory and practice of modern politics in all its dimensions.[19] In Strauss's view, Machiavelli was a conscious "teacher of evil" who deliberately undermined the classical teaching and brought about a "lowering of the standards of political life" by excluding questions about how people ought to live in favor of an emphasis on how they do live.[20] The revolution initiated by Machiavelli, which Strauss designates as the "first wave of modernity," was perpetuated by Hobbes who undertook to soften the harsh character of Machiavelli's teaching and to make its basic intention more capable of realization.[21] However, even "Hobbes's teaching was still much too bold to be acceptable. It too was in need of mitigation. The mitigation was the work of Locke."[22]

The second wave of modernity began with Rousseau.[23] Rousseau contributed to the growth of relativism by his acceptance of the general will as the criterion of moral and political judgment, and his project culminated in those philosophies of history characteristic of the nineteenth century. The failure of the grandiose visions of Hegel and Marx, which attempted to locate all meaning of political phenomena in the historical process, prepared the way for the contemporary epoch. This last wave was introduced by Nietzsche who, Strauss argues, is *"the* philosopher of relativism" and who established the intellectual foundations of existentialism and other aspects of the radical historicism that characterizes the modern age and the works of individuals such as Heidegger. Together, these three waves of modernity have resulted in the crisis of the present.[24]

ERIC VOEGELIN:
THE DERAILMENT OF POLITICAL THEORY

For Voegelin, as for Strauss, the study of the history of political philosophy is a form of "therapeutic analysis" that is demanded as a response to a modern intellectual and political crisis which threatens the West.[25] He insists that his work "should be read, not as an attempt to explore curiosities of a dead past, but as an inquiry into the structure of order in which we live presently" and as an attempt to regain a truth of political order that has been lost.[26] The task is one of "restoration" and "retheoretization."[27] This would return political science to the kind of enterprise founded by Plato and Aristotle and overcome the effects of positivism with its emphasis on emulating the methods of natural science and establishing a value-free mode of inquiry. This reflection on the past is required by "the spiritual disorder of our time, the civilizational crisis of which everyone so readily speaks."[28] But it is the experience of crisis which, as in all the great moments of political theory, makes possible this kind of historical reflection. Although we are living in an age of corruption, the "foundations of a new science of order have been laid" in response to the crisis. Through the development of modern historiography and an emancipation from "the ideological mortgages on the work of science," it is possible to extricate thought from the hold of positivism and the "morass of relativism" that characterized the last half of the nineteenth century and still persists in modern social science.[29] It is possible to create a science of politics that is in some sense comparable in scope and character to that of Aristotle.

In his major work, *Order and History,* Voegelin attempts to practice this science, or prepare the foundation for its practice. Here he elaborates his fundamental thesis: "the existence of man in political society is historical existence; and a theory of politics, if it penetrates to principles, must at the same time be a theory of history." Such a theory arises from an "exploration of the symbols by which political societies interpret themselves as representatives of a transcendent truth," and it demonstrates "an intelligible succession of phases in a historical process."[30] For Voegelin, "the order of history emerges from the history of order." While Western history does not reveal any precise pattern and the future is unknown, it is possible, within the limits of the present stage in the evolution of knowledge, to discern the basic process of man's search for the truth of social order and to identify the symbolic forms in which he has attempted to express that truth. Furthermore, it is possible to perceive, within the sequence of social orders, "advances toward, or recessions from, an adequate symbolization of truth concerning the order of being of which the order of society is a part."[31] The past is knowable as a reality that, retrospectively, emerges from the standpoint of the present. Voegelin maintains that he has been able to describe the principal types of order as they have emerged from the time of the civilizations of the ancient Near East to the appearance of the modern national state, and that he has succeeded in specifying and analyzing the symbols in which these orders have expressed themselves.

This historical process has included not only the discovery of philosophy but its degeneration, and Voegelin argues that "the history of philosophy is in the largest part the history of its derailment."[32] To specify the point and cause of this derailment and to recover the knowledge of the truth of existence and the kind of philosophical experience achieved prior to the derailment is the task he sets for himself. The modern crisis, which is the ultimate product of this intellectual derailment, can be solved only by a recapitulation and critique of those ideas that derived from the crucial point of the derailment of Western thought.

The modern crisis is, in Voegelin's view, the result of a Manichaean struggle between the corruptive forces of Gnosticism on one side and the remnants of true philosophy and rational politics on the other. "At present the fate is in the balance," and everywhere one may see the "manifestations of Gnostic insanity in the practice of contemporary politics."[33] From the English and American revolutions to those of France and Germany and finally Russia, the march of Gnosticism has continued in its left wing and right wing forms. The rise of national socialism and the Second World War as well as the postwar spread of communism and its less radical but still insidious expression, Western liberalism, which acquiesced in that spread, are all manifestations of Gnostic politics.[34] Sometimes Gnosticism expresses itself in intellectual movements and sometimes in political movements, and often there is a convergence. It includes progressivism, positivism, Hegelianism, Marxism, psychoanalysis, Communism, fascism, national socialism, and liberalism, and some of its most prominent representatives include Comte, Hegel, Marx, Nietzsche, and Heidegger.[35] Although Voegelin believes that to a limited degree an intellectual crack in the Gnostic ideology has deprived it of much of its authority and has allowed a critical examination of the modern crisis, the forces of Gnosticism still dominate contemporary politics. The question is, then, what exactly is Gnosticism?

Gnosticism usually refers to a diverse but widespread movement of the late pre-Christian and early Christian centuries that was based on claims to esoteric cosmic knowledge and which was derived from various Oriental, Jewish, and Christian sources. Gnostic doctrines were first espoused outside the church but later influenced Christian theology and were finally excluded as heretical by Christian orthodoxy. Voegelin rejects the idea that Gnosticism was merely a Christian heresy. He insists that it was a separate religious movement with a distinct theory of human existence and that there is an actual historical continuity between the beliefs of ancient Gnostic sects and modern political thought and action. Abstracting from the attributes of historical Gnosticism, he argues that the same basic ideas are visible in modern political philosophy. According to Gnosticism, Voegelin maintains, man is an alien in an evil world and seeks deliverance from and dominion over it through human knowledge and action. It is, in effect, the claim of man to be God or overcome God. Yet to fully understand Gnosticism, he argues, it is necessary to understand that against which it revolted.

Voegelin argues that "God and man, world and society form a primordial community of being."[36] During the course of history and the evolution of human consciousness, man's participation in this reality has been experienced and symbolized in different forms and with varying degrees or kinds of truth. *Order and History* traces this development. From the "cosmological" truth of the ancient myth and the ahistorical experience which characterized the civilizations of Egypt and Mesopotamia; to the "leap in being" that took place in Israel and Hellas and produced the awareness of human history and the distinction between society, God, and nature; to the Christian understanding of the relationship between man and God, there was a progressive symbolic differentiation. Through the revelatory experience of Israel, expressed by the Hebrew prophets, and the philosophical experience of Greece, characterized by the work of Plato and Aristotle, the community of being differentiated into immanent and transcendent orders of existence. However, the "anthropological" truth of Greek philosophy and its experience of the human soul attuned to an unseen order was, in Voegelin's view, a "mortgaged" Christianity. It was limited by its conception of individuals bound together in the political order of the polis as the means of human realization. This was succeeded by the "soteriological" truth of Christian revelation and its vision of a mutuality or friendship between God and humanity achieved through faith and grace.

For Voegelin, Greek philosophy, and particularly Christian revelation, were the apex of Western civilization's understanding of the truth of human existence. Here, he argues, was achieved the greatest differentiation of consciousness, and any retreat from this level of experience is necessarily an impoverishment and a "theoretical retrogression."[37] The criterion of maximum differentiation, and the attribution of this achievement to Greek and Christian thought, provides the basis of Voegelin's particular rendition of the evolution of Western political philosophy and a standard for distinguishing and evaluating the stages in this development.

The Gnostic derailment that Voegelin alleges is typified by what he takes to be a redivinization of man and society and a reintegration of immanence and transcendence which was already present in certain aspects of Christian and Jewish thought. He argues that while St. Augustine had emptied secular history of sacred or transcendent meaning, Joachim of Flora attempted to reendow the immanent course of mundane history with significance by transferring to it the symbols of Christian eschatology. He thereby "created the aggregate of symbols which govern the self-interpretation of modern political society to this day."[38] This was not an authentic return to the experience that characterized earlier forms of thought but rather a theoretical fallacy and deformation of symbols. This "attempt at immanentizing the meaning of existence"—or appropriating the symbols in which transcendence was experienced and applying them to an interpretation of human history—and this going beyond faith in order to seek final knowledge of man's nature and ultimate destiny and in order to prophesy the perfection of man and society in history is the essence of Gnosticism. It also constitutes "the inner logic of the Western political development from medieval immanentization through humanism, enlightenment, progressivism, liberalism, positivism, and Marxism," and finally it prepared the basis for the totalitarianism of the twentieth century.[39] Gnosticism involves the murder of God and the elimination of the experience of transcendence. In Voegelin's view, this has been a characteristic of the philosophies of history and politics from the Enlightenment to the present. This emulation of God is "the great dream that first appeared imaginatively in the works of Condorcet, Comte, Marx and Nietzsche and later pragmatically in the Communist and National Socialist movements."[40]

Voegelin thus claims to have discovered a "civilizational cycle of world-historic proportions. There emerge the contours of a giant cycle, transcending the cycles of the single civilization. The acme of the cycle would be marked by the appearance of Christ; the pre-Christian high civilizations would form its ascending branch; modern, Gnostic civilizations would form its descending branch."[41] It is within this scheme that Voegelin places the classic works of political theory, and it is within this vision of history that they gain their meaning and play their role.

HANNAH ARENDT:
THE DECLINE OF THE PUBLIC REALM

What Arendt mourns is not so much the decline of political philosophy as the decline of politics since, in her view, political philosophy was from its very origin inimical to politics. However, as political philosophy developed, it became yet more alienated from the original significance of the political dimension of life. Arendt undertakes an exploration of the debasement of the political by examining the path of Western political thought which, in her view, both reflected and contributed to its fate. For Arendt, the problem of the modern age is manifest in totalitarianism as well as in the conformism and materialism of behavior in liberal democratic mass society. However, these are symptoms of a deeper malaise and a "general crisis that has overtaken the modern world"—a crisis which centers around the contraction and degeneration of the political or public realm and the loss of traditional authority as well as the authority of the tradition.[42]

Arendt maintains that in the modern age "the gap between past and future," in which political thought is always forced to move, is no longer bridged by tradition as it had been ever since "Roman civilization submitted to the authority of Greek thought."[43] In the modern age, when the continuity of the tradition was broken, man found himself in a condition of intellectual and political confusion.[44] Modern man was unprepared for this situation which became "desperate" when he realized "that he had come to live in a world in which his mind and his tradition of thought were not even capable of asking adequate, meaningful questions, let alone of giving answers to its own perplexities."[45] However, although the loss of the tradition has created the danger of forgetting the past, it has also created the possibility of a new self-consciousness and an opportunity to recover what the past had forgotten.

Through a "critical interpretation of the past" it is possible "to discover the real origins of traditional concepts in order to distill from them anew their original spirit which has so sadly evaporated from the very key words of political language."[46] With the break in the tradition, there is now the possibility that the past will "open up to us with unexpected freshness and tell us things no one has yet had ears to hear," and "implicit in it is the great chance to look upon the past with eyes undisturbed by a tradition, with a directness which has disappeared from Occidental reading and hearing."[47] Arendt maintains that "the beginning and the end of the tradition have this in common: that the elementary problems of politics never come as clearly to light in their immediate and simple urgency as when they are first formulated and when they receive their final challenge."[48] She argues that "the purpose of the historical analysis is to trace back modern world alienation . . . to its origins, in order to arrive at an understanding of the nature of society as it had developed and presented itself at the very moment when it was overcome by the advent of a new and yet unknown age."[49] The purpose is practical; the aim is to rewaken a sense of the value of the political as a dimension of life and to reveal the source of the modern crisis.

Arendt insists that the tradition of political thought that began with Plato and Aristotle was finally destroyed by such philosophers of the modern age as Kierkegaard, Marx, and Nietzsche. In her view, this was a matter of a "conscious rebellion" that was more a revolution within the tradition than against it.[50] It involved an inversion of the values of traditional politics rather than the creation of new values. The rebels brought the tradition to an end but did not manage to extricate themselves from its categories, and thus found themselves trying "desperately to think against the tradition while using its own conceptual tools."[51] The tradition ran dry. However, although the collapse of the tradition brought us "to the threshold of a radical nihilism," she denies that either the vitiation of the tradition or the intellectual chaos that followed it "actually caused the break in our history."[52] Rather "this sprang from a chaos of mass-perplexities on the political scene and of mass-opinions in the spiritual sphere which the totalitarian movements, through terror and ideology, crystalized into a new form of government and domination."[53] The rebels tried within the framework of the tradition to confront the problems of the new age with which that framework was unable to cope, and their failure, their inability to do more than turn the tradition upside down, has produced the intellectual crisis of the modern age. Yet, this crisis does at last make it possible to escape the tradition and gain a nontraditional perspective on the problem of man in political society by a historical recovery of pretraditional ideas.

Although the tradition, in each successive stage, brought Western man further away from the original meaning of politics and "became destructive as it came to its end," the tradition of political theory did not begin simply as a confrontation with a particular political regime, that of ancient Athens, but with a critique of politics itself.[54] She maintains that "our philosphical tradition of political thought, beginning with Parmenides and Plato, was founded explicitly in opposition to the polis and its citizenry" and with "the philosopher's turning away from politics and then returning in order to impose his standards on human affairs."[55] It is as an idealized reconstruction of the institutions and values of the Greek polis and Periclean Athens that Arendt explicates the concept of the political or public realm, undertakes her interpretation of the history of politics and political philosophy, and judges the condition of politics in the modern age. The classical polis, in her view, properly reflected the requirements of human existence.

Arendt declines to postulate a substantive concept of human nature, but she does believe that it is possible to isolate the basic structures of the human condition to which political experience should conform. What she designates as the *vita activa* consists of labor, work, and action. Labor corresponds to the biological level of existence or the life-preserving processes of the individual and species which human beings have in common with all animals. Through work, humans transcend nature by creating artifacts that persist through time and compensate in some respect for the transience of mortal life. Yet it is action that embodies the most distinctly human capacities and faculties such as speech. Action involves a plurality of individuals engaged in public activity, and it is the condition of all political life as well as the basis of history. However, political space—the political order and the life of the citizen—is also the condition of action. Human beings literally create themselves as individuals through action, and when a realm of significant action and the possibility of distinguishing oneself in public is denied, the essential character of human being is truncated and a basic dimension of human freedom is eliminated. Arendt argues that the classical Greek polis, as represented by the values associated with individuals such as Pericles and as analyzed by Aristotle, represented a particular, and correct, ordering of the *vita activa*. Here the priority of the public realm over other aspects of human existence was recognized. The history of political philosophy, as well as politics, has been the history of the reversal of that hierarchy and the distortion of the demands of the human condition.

According to Arendt, that the Greeks equated the *vita activa* with the *bios politikos* demonstrated the primacy they gave to action or the public dimension of social life. The polis provided the public space in which free and equal citizens, by word and deed, sought a measure of immortality through fame preserved in the communal memory. The other basic dimension of life, the private sphere of economics and family involving the life-sustaining activities, was considered ancillary and subservient to public concerns. Private life constituted the material base which supported political life. In her view, even legislation, city-building, and government in general, were construed as instrumental to the ends and possibilities of political action and as basically prepolitical.

Only for this one golden moment in history did politics attain its right place in the scheme of human life. With the decline of Athens, the Socratic school turned away from *praxis* or action and toward *poiesis* or making. They embraced political artifice informed by philosophy as an answer to political problems. They turned "against politics and against action . . . as though they said that if men only renounce their capacity for action, with its futility, boundlessness, and uncertainty of outcome, there could be a remedy for the frailty of human affairs."[56] For Plato, the proper constitution of the good city would obviate the need for creative political action and hold politics within severe intellectual and physical constraints. In addition, the philosopher ultimately sought the realization of the self outside and beyond the city in a life dedicated to the contemplation of the eternal (*theoria*). It was against the authority of an eternal order discovered by reason that the philosopher measured human action, and he wished to transform the *vita activa* in accordance with the authority of this transcendent standard. The life of the citizen, or the *bios politikos,* was demoted to an inferior status and viewed as contradictory to the life of the philosopher or the *vita contemplativa.* The idea of immortality achieved through political action and the memory of the citizenry gave way, in the philosophical tradition of thought, to the striving for eternity achieved through contemplation. Arendt suggests that "the greater part of political philosophy since Plato could easily be interpreted as various attempts to find theoretical foundations and practical ways for an escape from politics altogether," and Christianity merely "conferred a religious sanction upon the abasement of the *vita activa* to its derivative, secondary position."[57]

In the modern age, and in modern political philosophy, there was a reversal of what had come to be understood as the traditional relationship between the *vita contemplativa* and the *vita activa,* that is, the ranking of theory over practice or thought over action. However the ascendancy of doing over knowing, and the idea of the latter as an instrument of the former, did not involve a return to the ideas of the polis and the reinstatement of the priority of political action, since it had been preceded by a reversal of priorities within the *vita activa* itself. Work, or "making," and the idea of man as *homo faber* had gained preeminence over politics and become the defining characteristic of human activity. This development, however, had its roots in the very beginnings of political philosophy. In addition to the Platonic suspicion of political action, there was, Arendt maintains, a fundamental complementarity between the philosopher's search for the eternal as a paradigm of order and standard of judgment and the craftsman's concern with permanence and the replication of a model; "contemplation and fabrication (*theoria* and *poiesis*) have an inner affinity and do not stand in the same unequivocal opposition to each other as contemplation and action."[58] Yet still more important for understanding our present intellectual situation is the fact that the elevation of *homo faber* was rapidly followed by a second intellectual inversion which brought labor to the top of the hierarchy within the *vita activa.*

This last development in Western thought, which most directly ushered in the modern age, was made possible largely by "the introduction of the concept of process into making." The emphasis on the "fabrication process" entailed a depreciation of the concern with the permanence of the product and a permanent guiding model that had heretofore characterized both theory and making.[59] Human beings came to be defined in terms of process and as part of the processes of history and nature. The rise of the modern concept of history and the idea of the historical process in the eighteenth century was accompanied by a "concomitant decrease in purely political thinking" which eventually culminated in "Marx's identification of action with 'the making of history.' "[60] As *animal laborans,* human beings were no longer understood as immortalizing through action in the classical sense. Instead, they were identified with the idea of life itself, and the perpetuation of the natural life process of the species came to be viewed as the highest good of human activity. What for the Greeks constituted necessity and privatization and sustained the possibility of the exercise of the higher faculties of human being became, for Marx, the end of human existence, while making and doing, as well as knowing, became its means. For Arendt, Marx's thought accomplished in a substantive sense the intellectual revolution he had effected symbolically when he as "a philosopher turned away from philosophy so as to 'realize' it in politics."[61]

The tradition ended with the demise of a distinctly public realm, the reduction of politics to government, and the rise of society as the basic concept of human interaction. For Marx, as well as for modern social science, both thought and action, or philosophy and politics, became "mere functions of society and history."[62] For Arendt, the Marxian idea of human beings as social and historical animals constituted the complete reversal of the Western political tradition, yet, she suggests, Marx "in this as in other respects only summed up, conceptualized, and transformed into a program the underlying assumptions of two hundred years of modernity."[63]

SHELDON WOLIN:
THE SUBLIMATION OF POLITICS

Wolin, like Strauss, is concerned with the decline of political philosophy and, like Arendt, with what he believes to be the concurrent decline, or loss of identity, of the political realm. However, his account of the fall of the tradition is somewhat less schematic and romantic than the previous three writers. He is much more concerned with demonstrating that what is studied is in fact an actual historical tradition and a particular "intellectual enterprise"[64] and that the study of the tradition, as well as the mode of thought that constituted the tradition, are facing a crucial challenge from contemporary political and social science.

Wolin argues that the history of political theory is the history of "a special tradition of discourse" and that it is possible to analyze it as a distinct and concrete "activity whose characteristics are most clearly revealed over time" and to identify the "acknowledged masters" who have contributed to its development.[65] For Wolin, political theory or political philosophy is a particular species of philosophy or the search for "systematic knowledge," and the difference is largely a "matter of specialization." Also, he suggests that there is an affinity between political philosophy and philosophy in general in that they have a common concern with the public. Philosophy seeks public knowledge, and political philosophy seeks knowledge about public things.[66] It is this concern with the character of the political realm, including both its boundaries and content, that is at the center of "the continuity of preoccupations" which constitutes the tradition. Wolin maintains that, in large measure, what is taken to be political, how it is conceived, and the concepts and categories in terms of which it is discussed "are the legacy accruing from the historical activity of political philosophers."[67] Therefore, an understanding of the tradition becomes essential for an understanding of contemporary politics and how it is perceived and discussed.

Wolin believes that political philosophy can be defined as a continuing dialogue on the problem of how "to render politics compatible with the requirements of order," that is, how to reconcile the conflict created by competition under conditions of scarcity with the demands of public tranquility.[68] Wolin notes that the vision of the philosopher is usually a response to a crisis in political society and that it constitutes an imaginative reconstruction of politics that reflects his diagnosis of social ills. In elaborating his vision, the philosopher is always to some extent constrained by the concepts, institutional facts, and self-defined problems of society, but, "of all the restraints upon the political philosopher's freedom to speculate, none has been so powerful as the tradition of political philosophy itself."[69]

Central to Wolin's argument about the tradition is the thesis

that "most formal political speculation has operated simultaneously at two different levels. At one level every political philosopher has concerned himself with what he thinks to be a vital problem of his day. . . . At another level, however, many political
writings . . . have been meant as a contribution to the continuing dialogue of Western political philosophy."[70] There are thus two
levels of intention that must be addressed when interpreting a
classic work, and the principal one involves the theorist's self-conscious concern "to participate in the perennial dialogue" and to
"contribute to the tradition of Western political speculation."[71]
Thus, for example, what is essential in understanding Locke is his
intention to refute Hobbes, and as important as the historical circumstances of sixteenth century Italy may be for interpreting
Machiavelli's work, the context of the great tradition and its dialogue is more important. No matter how great his attempt at innovation, "the theorist enters into a debate the terms of which have
largely been set beforehand" and thus becomes a participant in the
tradition of political thought which forms a "cultural legacy" or
"inherited body of knowledge" that binds together past and present political experience and provides a means of accommodating
to the future.[72] However, both the political realm and the tradition
of political philosophy are in trouble in the modern age.

Wolin argues that both politics and political philosophy had a
quite definite beginning in ancient Greece. "It is to the Greeks that
we are indebted for the invention of political philosophy and for the
demarcation of the area of political nature."[73] Like Arendt, Wolin
believes that politics and political philosophy emerged in confrontation. Plato's vision was "sworn to an eternal hostility towards politics," and his plan for society called for an elimination of political
action in favor of the imposition of a unity based on a transcendent
and nonpolitical model of order.[74] Aristotle, on the other hand,
predicated his analysis much more on the actual "nature of political phenomena" and succeeded in articulating many of their principal features.[75] Although Wolin insists "that the field of politics is
and has been, in a significant and radical sense, a created one," and
not something "written into the nature of things," he maintains
that "the adjective 'political' has had a more or less stable mean-

ing" throughout the tradition of Western political thought and that this meaning was to a large extent first enunciated by Aristotle.[76] For Wolin, political refers to the sphere of public judgments— those which are backed by the authority of the community, applicable to the community as a whole, and arrived at through a process of participation involving the various kinds of legitimate claims recognized by the political association. However, this realm has contracted, expanded, and in various ways changed in both form and content over time, and political philosophy has sometimes responded to such changes and at other times acted as a catalyst.

The decline of the Greek polis and its absorption into the empires of the ancient world brought about a decline of political philosophy, since it "deprived political thought of its basic unit of analysis" and transformed political philosophy "into a species of moral philosophy."[77] Despite the obvious inherent tension between the worldly demands of politics and the other-worldly orientation of religion, "it fell to Christianity to revivify political thought" by establishing "a new and powerful ideal of community" and by appropriating political tactics and political symbols in realizing its own goals.[78] "Political thought was nourished and extended through the middle ages," and Christian thinkers such as St. Augustine and St. Thomas Aquinas, in their attempt to specify and differentiate the character of political as opposed to religious concerns and to clarify the relation between church and state, unwittingly provided the intellectual basis for "Machiavelli's reassertion of the radical autonomy of political order"—"the first great experiment in a 'pure' political theory."[79] This was followed, and complemented, by Hobbes's theory of the secular foundations of political authority and his vision of the construction of a political order out of the material of discrete, asocial, self-interested, power-seeking individuals.

After Hobbes, there began the second great decline of political philosophy that has carried forward to the present. This decline is the result "of a condition where the sense of the political has been lost," and this in turn is paradoxically in large part the consequence of the fact that "the main trends in political thought . . . have worked towards the same end: the erosion of the distinctly political" and its displacement by the social.[80] This was accomplished by two basic subtraditions in Western political thought. One emanated from the assortment of thinkers from Montesquieu to de Tocqueville who explained political institutions, ideas, and authority as a functional superstructure resting on various social relationships and private associations. The other intellectual development, growing out of the work of Locke, utilitarianism, and classical liberalism, identified the political narrowly with government and viewed it as a limited but necessary artificial and coercive instrument for serving society and its prior natural interests. These developments gradually led to a displacement of politics in favor of society, of political theory in favor of social science. The conditions of the modern age and the trends of contemporary thought have given "rise to two closely interrelated problems. . . . They are the problems of community and organization" or those of how to create community in an age of organization.[81] This has involved a search for a social answer to social problems and the neglect of politics.

Wolin argues that there has been a loss of a sense of the distinctiveness, primacy, and generality of the political or public realm in human life or what he describes as "the sublimation of the political into forms of association which earlier thought had believed to be non-political."[82] At the same time, what was once thought to be nonpolitical has been politicized. The political is at once everywhere and nowhere, and it has been dissected, dispersed, and absorbed by society. Political thought has both suffered from and contributed to this situation. Wolin maintains that the problems of the modern age can be solved only by a reawakening of the sense of the political and a revitalization of political theory. Ultimately "human existence is not going to be decided at the lesser level of small associations: it is the political order that is making fateful decisions about man's survival in an age haunted by the possibility of unlimited destruction."[83]

For Wolin, the study of the history of political theory is required to "rescue" political philosophy and recapture the original sense of the political. A "historical perspective is more effective than any other in exposing the nature of our present predicaments; if it is not the source of political wisdom, it is at least the precondition."[84] In addition to seeking an explanation of the present in the tradition, "the study of the historical development of that tradition" provides a "grammar and vocabulary to facilitate communication and orient understanding" with regard to politics and political thought. Further, "since the history of political philosophy is . . . an intellectual development wherein successive thinkers have added new dimensions to the analysis and understanding of politics, an inquiry into that development is not so much a venture into antiquarianism as a form of political education."[85]

Wolin had set out to defend the study of the history of political theory in the face of "marked hostility towards, and even contempt for, political philosophy in its traditional form," and it is by writing the history of political theory as a form of education that he responds to the kind of attack that was mounted by Easton against the irrelevance of the enterprise.[86] Like Strauss, Wolin sees contemporary political science, with its pretensions regarding the emulation of the natural sciences, its "historyless" orientation, and its obsession with method in empirical inquiry, as a powerful educational institution. Yet it is one that has depreciated and jeopardized "political wisdom" or the "tacit political knowledge" which develops over time and is "so vital to making judgments, not only about the adequacy and value of theories and methods, but about the nature and perplexities of politics as well."[87] Wolin tends to oppose scientific and traditional political theory and identify the former with "methodism" in contemporary social science, but he takes pains to point out, drawing heavily upon Thomas Kuhn's work in the history of science, that the conception of scientific activity and its history held by social scientists is very inadequate. In many respects, there are significant parallels between scientific theory and the evolution of scientific paradigms on the one hand and traditional political philosophy and its transformations on the other hand. Both natural science and political philosophy are creative intellectual endeavors, and a historical understanding of their character and development is instructive.[88]

Wolin contrasts the enterprise of the methodist, characteristic of contemporary political science, with the "vocation" of the political theorist or those who preserve our understanding of past theories, who sharpen our sense of the subtle, complex interplay between political experience and thought, and who preserve our memory of the agonizing efforts of intellect to restate the possibilities and threats posed by political dilemmas of the past. In teaching about past theories, the historically-minded theorist is engaged in the task of political initiation, that is, of introducing new generations of students to the complexities of politics and to the efforts of theorists to confront its predicaments; of developing the capacity for discriminating judgments . . . and of cultivating that sense of 'significance' which . . . is vital to scientific inquiry but cannot be furnished by scientific methods; and of exploring the ways in which new theoretical vistas are opened.[89]

However, even if the political theorist as historian might succeed, in some measure, in keeping the tradition alive within the inimical climate created by social science, there are severe problems for a continuation of the "epic" tradition that has existed since Plato and for the preservation of that "vocation by which political theories are created."[90] The character of the *bios theoretikos* and the intentions that informed it seem singularly irrelevant in the modern world which is the product of rational human design and technology, rather than historical evolution, and which, with its "giant, routinized structures," is "impervious to theory." The world "shows increasing signs of coming apart" and our social condition "threatens to become anomalous," and "yet amidst this chaos political science exudes a complacency which beggars description" and thus exacerbates the modern plight.[91] Ultimately Wolin appears to be pessimistic about the regeneration of traditional political philosophy and resigned to the task of keeping the memory of the tradition alive and demonstrating its practical relevance or, failing that, at least "making clear what it is we shall have discarded."[92]

CONCLUSION

In each of these writers there is an overwhelming dominance of common concerns and patterns of argument that justifies treating this literature as a relatively distinct genre. The basic premises of these arguments are so similar, and so widely accepted, that their existence and character are sometimes obscured. Although the particular views on politics and the tradition may differ to some degree and Wolin, for example, may charge Strauss and his followers with propagating a brand of political education that limits our choices to either a "morally corrupt and intellectually sterile scientism or a version of political philosophy distinguished by a moral fervor and an intellectual certainty that the essential nature of all political situations has been revealed long ago," this is definitely an interspecific debate.[93] The subtleties would be hardly apparent to the uninitiated. The differences are in many respects not unlike, and maybe not as great as, those between certain schools of psychoanalysis regarding the methods of diagnosis and treatment.

What is more significant than any disagreement is the consensus on such matters as the historical reality of the tradition; the identification of its major participants and their role in the development or decline of the tradition; the points of the inception and demise of the tradition; the reverence for the Greeks, particularly Aristotle, and the beginning of the tradition; the aversion to modern philosophy and individuals such as Heidegger; the disclaimer of any purely antiquarian interests; the insistence on the crucial relevance of historical studies; the emphasis on the tradition as a principal factor in explaining the present; the antipathy toward contemporary political and social science and its status as a rival educational instrument; the concern with the deficiencies of modern liberalism; the existence, and basic characteristics of, the modern crisis; the sense in which the crisis frees thought for a critique of the tradition; the overall pattern of the tradition as one of decline; the basic division between ancient and modern segments of the tradition and the critique of modernity; the rise of the social over the political realm in the course of the tradition; the sense in which the tradition developed the seeds of its own destruction; and the role of the historian as the transmitter and preserver of political wisdom and the remnant of political theory in the modern age.

In both form and content, there are pervasive similarities among these works, and these similarities have been transformed

into a series of regulative assumptions which have come to dominate the history of political theory as a field of study. What is important is that in these works *the idea of the tradition* has been
articulated, elaborated, and finally transformed into what must be
termed *the myth of the tradition*. This myth demands careful
scrutiny before there can be any clear understanding or reasonable
assessment of the character of contemporary scholarship in the
history of political theory.

NOTES

1. John H. Hallowell, *Main Currents in Modern Political Thought*
(New York: Henry Holt, 1950), p. 12.

2. Leo Strauss, *The City and Man* (Chicago: Rand McNally, 1964),
p. 1.

3. Leo Strauss, *What is Political Philosophy?* (Glencoe, Ill.: Free
Press, 1959), pp. 56–59.

4. Strauss, *The City and Man,* p. 1.

5. Ibid., pp. 2–3; Leo Strauss, "Political Philosophy and the Crisis of
Our Time," in George J. Graham, Jr. and George W. Carey, eds. *The Post-
Behavioral Era* (New York: David McKay, 1972), p. 242; Leo Strauss,
"Relativism," in Helmut Schoeck and James W. Wiggins, eds., *Relativism
and the Study of Man* (Princeton: D. VanNostrand, 1961), p. 140; Leo
Strauss, *Natural Right and History* (Chicago: University of Chicago
Press, 1953), pp. 5–6.

6. Strauss, *What is Political Philosophy?*, pp. 11–12.

7. Strauss, "Introduction," in Leo Strauss and Joseph Cropsey,
eds., *History of Political Philosophy* (Chicago: Rand McNally, 1963), p.
2; Strauss, *What is Political Philosophy?*, p. 17.

8. Strauss, *What is Political Philosophy?*, p. 18.

9. Ibid., pp. 20, 25–27, 57; Strauss, *Natural Right and History*, pp.
4, 18–19.

10. Leo Strauss, "Epilogue," in Herbert J. Storing, ed., *Essays on the
Scientific Study of Politics* (New York: Holt, Rinehart and Winston,
1962), pp. 307, 319–27; Leo Strauss, *On Tyranny* (New York: Free Press,
1963), p. 22.

11. Strauss, *Natural Right and History,* p. 7.

12. Ibid., p. 31.

13. Strauss, *The City and Man,* p. 9.

14. Strauss, *What is Political Philosophy?,* p. 67.

15. Strauss, *The City and Man,* p. 10; "Epilogue," p. 313.

16. Strauss, *What is Political Philosophy?,* pp. 68–69.

17. Ibid., pp. 27, 54.

18. Strauss, "Political Philosophy and the Crisis of Our Time," pp. 217–18.

19. Strauss, *On Tyranny,* pp. 23, 110–11; *What is Political Philosophy?,* p. 40.

20. Strauss, *What is Political Philosophy?,* p. 41; Leo Strauss, *Thoughts on Machiavelli* (Glencoe, Ill.: Free Press, 1958), pp. 9, 13.

21. Strauss, *What is Political Philosophy?,* pp. 47–48.

22. Ibid., p. 49.

23. Ibid., p. 50.

24. Strauss, "Relativism," p. 151; *What is Political Philosophy?,* p. 54.

25. Eric Voegelin, *Science, Politics and Gnosticism* (Chicago: Henry Regnery, 1968), p. 23.

26. Eric Voegelin, *Order and History,* vol. 1, *Israel and Revelation* (Baton Rouge: Louisiana State University Press, 1956), p. xiv.

27. Eric Voegelin, *The New Science of Politics* (Chicago: University of Chicago Press, 1952), pp. 1, 3, 5; *Science, Politics and Gnosticism,* p. 15.

28. Voegelin, *The New Science of Politics,* p. 5; *Science, Politics and Gnosticism,* p. 22.

29. Voegelin, *Science, Politics and Gnosticism,* p. 6; *Order and History,* vol. 3, *Plato and Aristotle* (Baton Rouge: Louisiana State University Press, 1957), p. 357; *Israel and Revelation,* p. xii; *The New Science of Politics,* pp. 13, 26.

30. Voegelin, *The New Science of Politics,* p. 1.

31. Voegelin, *Israel and Revelation,* p. ix.

32. Voegelin, *Plato and Aristotle,* p. 277.

33. Voegelin, *The New Science of Politics,* pp. 189, 170–71.

34. Ibid., pp. 171–89.

35. Voegelin, *Science, Politics and Gnosticism,* pp. v, 83.

36. Voegelin, *Israel and Revelation,* p. 1.

37. Voegelin, *The New Science of Politics,* pp. 79–80.

38. Ibid., p. 111.

39. Ibid., p. 125.

40. Eric Voegelin, *From Enlightenment to Revolution* (Durham: Duke University Press, 1975), p. 302.

41. Voegelin, *The New Science of Politics,* p. 164.

42. Hannah Arendt, *Between Past and Future* (New York: Viking, 1961), pp. 173, 140.

43. Ibid., pp. 13, 49.

44. Ibid., pp. 14, 18.

45. Ibid., pp. 8–9.

46. Ibid., p. 15.

47. Ibid., pp. 29, 94.

48. Ibid., p. 18.

49. Hannah Arendt, *The Human Condition* (New York: Doubleday, 1958), pp. 6–7.

50. Arendt, *Between Past and Future,* pp. 21, 31.

51. Ibid., pp. 18, 25–26.

52. Ibid., pp. 26, 34.

53. Ibid., p. 26.

54. Ibid., p. 18.

55. Ibid., pp. 18, 150; also *The Human Condition,* p. 13.

56. Arendt, *The Human Condition,* p. 174.

57. Ibid., pp. 16, 198.

58. Ibid., p. 275.

59. Ibid., pp. 274, 278, 280.

60. Arendt, *Between Past and Future,* pp. 76–77.

61. Ibid., p. 18.

62. Ibid., p. 30.

63. Arendt, *The Human Condition,* p. 55.

64. Sheldon S. Wolin, *Politics and Vision* (Boston: Little, Brown, 1960), p. v.

65. Ibid., pp. 1–2.

66. Ibid., pp. 2–3.

67. Ibid., pp. 3, 5.

68. Ibid., pp. 10–11.

69. Ibid., p. 22.

70. Ibid., p. 25.

71. Ibid., pp. 22, 26.

72. Ibid., pp. 22–23.

73. Ibid., p. 28.

74. Ibid., pp. 42–43.

75. Ibid., p. 59.

76. Ibid., pp. 5, 61.

77. Ibid., p. 94.

78. Ibid., pp. 96–97.

79. Ibid., pp. 137, 139, 198.

80. Ibid., pp. 288, 290.

81. Ibid., p. 363.

82. Ibid., p. 429.

83. Ibid., p. 434.

84. Sheldon S. Wolin, *Natural Law Forum* 5 (1960): 177; *Politics and Vision,* p. v.

85. Wolin, *Politics and Vision,* p. 27.

86. Ibid., p. v.

87. Sheldon S. Wolin, "Political Theory as a Vocation," *American Political Science Review* 63 (December 1969): 1070–71, 1077.

88. See Wolin, "Political Theory as a Vocation," and "Paradigms and Political Theories," in Preston King and B. C. Parekh, eds., *Politics and Experience* (Cambridge: Cambridge University Press, 1968).

89. Wolin, "Political Theory as a Vocation," p. 1077.

90. Sheldon S. Wolin, *Hobbes and the Epic Tradition of Political Theory* (Los Angeles: William Andrews Clark Memorial Library, University of California, 1970), p. 4; "Political Theory as a Vocation," p. 1078.

91. Wolin, "Political Theory as a Vocation," p. 1081.

92. Wolin, *Politics and Vision,* p. v.

93. John H. Schaar and Sheldon S. Wolin, "Essays on the Scientific Study of Politics: A Critique," *American Political Science Review* 57 (March 1963): 150.

Karl Marx   1818–1883

III

The Myth of the Tradition

> . . . to do this is to give up the story-teller's concern
> with the topical and the transitory and to endow oc-
> currences with a potency they cannot have without
> surrendering their character as occurrences. It is not
> to tell a story but to construct a myth.
>
> *Oakeshott*

THE USES OF THE TRADITION

The idea of the tradition is not so much a research conclusion as it is an *a priori* concept. It has come to inform the interpretation of particular works both in that they are viewed as elements of a tradition and in that a meaning is attributed to them which derives from a particular construction of the tradition as a whole and its implications for the present. I do not wish to suggest that there is no such thing as a Western tradition of politics and political ideas or that there are no discernible traditions of political thought. Neither do I wish to imply that there are no grounds for considering collectively the works usually taken as constituting the tradition. The point is not to deny that these works are important products of Western culture or that they in some way, individually or together, illuminate our past and present. They deserve consideration from various perspectives (literary, historical, and philosophical), and they surely are part of a heritage that comes to us through various traditions of education and scholarship. As with any such heritage, they carry authoritative prescriptions which require critical examination and openness. Nevertheless, I do insist that what is usually taken to be *the* tradition as elaborated by individuals such as Strauss, Voegelin, Arendt, and Wolin is a myth. The conventional sequence of classic works is not the core of any specific inherited pattern of thought that informs contemporary politics, and the substantive character with which these critics endow this corpus is a fiction. The assumption that there is in fact such a tradition is simply a mistake, and there are few greater interpretive prejudices than the unreflective approach to particular works in political theory as if they were elements of such a tradition.

The myth of the tradition has in large measure been the result of the practical or instrumental concerns which have governed the approach of historians of political theory. I wish neither to suggest

that a critical attitude toward the past or present is in some way illegitimate nor to defend some version of the thesis that the only
valid posture for the historian of ideas is one of disinterested interpretation for its own sake. However when scholarship in the history of political theory serves principally to attack the philosophical
foundations of contemporary political thought and action and to
critically assess social science, it often becomes difficult to distinguish interpretation and critique. This literature is instrumental
not only in that it is directed toward an explanation and evaluation
of the present rather than an illumination of the past, but in that
interpretations of particular works are viewed principally as a
means of reconstructing the tradition as a whole. It is perfectly
reasonable to distinguish between an interpretation of a work and
the purpose for which the interpretation is undertaken, and the
former is not necessarily dependent on the latter. Furthermore,
the validity of an interpretation of a text is not necessarily dependent on the validity of an account of the tradition in which that text
supposedly figures. Yet in the historical commentaries under consideration here, these issues are not separable and, in many respects, one would badly misconstrue much of this literature by
attempting to disjoin them. These general reconstructions of the
tradition as well as the interpretations of particular works are to a
large extent intelligible only in view of the reasons for which they
are undertaken, and the degree to which these interpretations
function as part of an overall argument about the character of the
tradition and the pathology of modern politics is too apparent to be
ignored.

To assume that this literature is simply a species of the history
of ideas would, despite the great ambiguity about the criteria for
judging scholarship in that field and notwithstanding the historical

form of the argument, distort the nature of the enterprise and obscure what these authors are doing. What is presented is not so much intellectual history as an epic tale, with heroes and villains, which is designed to lend authority to a diagnosis of the deficiencies of the present. The past is often used in very much the same manner as a dramatist might use events of everyday life to construct the world of the play. One might suggest that ultimately all history is an interpretation of the past in light of the present, but the question here is not simply one of the historical truth of the claims but rather what kind of activity is engaged in and what intentions inform it. The existence of the tradition is not something which is demonstrated in these works but something which the authors assume, or at least count on their audience assuming. The characterization of the course of the tradition presupposes the existence of the tradition. Little or no attempt is made to offer evidence that the diverse works from Plato to Marx actually constitute an inherited pattern of thought with causal implications for contemporary politics and political ideas, and the very concept of a tradition is seldom explicated in any precise and full manner. Any account of the historical relationships between the ideas of the figures who constitute the putative tradition or an explanation of their impact on politics is seldom offered. Yet the existence of such connections would be crucial for supporting the ostensible claims of this literature.

Each of these historians may articulate a somewhat distinctive tradition myth, but the principal features of the myth of the tradition are apparent in much of the literature on the history of political theory. Over the years, by academic convention, a basic repertoire of works has been selected, arranged chronologically, represented as an actual historical tradition, infused with evolutionary meaning, laden with significance derived from various symbolic themes and motifs, and offered up as the intellectual antecedents of contemporary politics and political thought. Arguments within the field of the history of political theory have become principally arguments about the meaning of this tradition, its implications for the present, and the place of particular works in the development of the tradition. Although certain works, such as those of Plato, Machiavelli, and Hobbes, are nearly always considered as given or essential elements of the tradition, the criteria of inclusion and the distribution of emphasis tend to depend on a prior conception of the structure and meaning of the tradition as a whole.

Despite obvious textual and contextual differences between the work of various classic authors, that is, the great disparities in literary form, historical circumstances, and purpose as well as temporal distance that separate, for example, Plato's *Republic* and Machiavelli's *Prince,* these works are approached in a manner that assumes, or would lead the reader to assume, that they may be understood as if they belonged to a common genre and as if their concern, as viewed from their own perspective, were with a common set of issues and ideas. The presumption is that these works are the residue of a historically specifiable activity characterized by relatively persistent and stable concerns, and that its recognizable temporal career can be charted by moving from the work of one paradigmatic figure to that of another. It is suggested that these works may be fruitfully understood, quite literally, as a continuing dialogue regarding the great perennial issues of political life and that the differences between these works may be conceived as innovations in the tradition and the similarities may be construed as continuities. Although there are considerable differences between the accounts offered by various historians about the precise content, meaning, direction, and impact of the tradition, there is, as I attempted to demonstrate in the last chapter, a significant structural similarity in their arguments and a definite convergence of their definitions of the modern crisis and the ideas and events that precipitated it.

While earlier historians such as Dunning and Sabine saw, despite some aberrations, a generally progressive development toward scientific knowledge and democracy, later writers such as Strauss, Voegelin, Arendt, and Wolin concur in the view that modernity and its conception of science and politics is the terminus of a tradition that has brought the West to a profound social and intellectual crisis. They claim to be engaged in a historical exploration that seeks to locate the origins of the modern crisis and prepare the way for a critical reassessment of contemporary politics. The specific intellectual grounds of these synoptic visions of the tradition may differ considerably, but, whatever their ultimate foundation, they are all part of, and continue to contribute to, what have become the dominant assumptions in the study of the history of political theory.

What is presented as a historical tradition is in fact basically a retrospective analytical construction which constitutes a rationalized version of the past. It evokes a certain image of our collective political mind and the political condition of our age, if not the human condition itself. It is history presented in cosmic dimensions. When it comes to the interpretation of particular works, they are inevitably, to a large degree, approached and understood in terms of their assigned role in this reconstructed tradition and in terms of assumptions about politics and the nature of the activity of political theory. Further, political theory, as both action and product, is an ideal typification based, often, on an extrapolation from Greek political thought as well as certain general characteristics of the other classic works. This abstract model is then reified and discussed as if it were a concrete and historically delimited activity in which individuals self-consciously addressed themselves to standard philosophical problems relating to the foundations of political life. The chosen works, viewed as exemplifications of political theory, are presented as a tradition which is then analyzed in terms of its beginning, transformation, end, or revival. It then becomes possible to advance what seem to be empirical, rather than merely categorical, claims about its structure and qualitative features. What emerges is a historical drama, but its import depends initially on the predisposition of the audience to accept the reality of the tradition.

This approach may not be significantly different from certain modes of historical criticism and interpretative analysis in philosophy, literature, and other fields, and my concern is not to suggest that this kind of commentary is illegitimate. Yet the problem is that the vehicle, that is, the idea of the tradition, has begun to take on a life of its own and that those who employ this form of analysis have sometimes become captives of their own invention. There is also a propensity for others, both students and scholars, to accept it without understanding its implications or the intentions of its creators. During the twentieth century, the idea of the tradition gained an existence independent of the concerns that gave rise to it, and the historians of political theory who have been most influential in the past two or three decades have appropriated the idea of the tradition and transformed it into the myth of the tradition. For many scholars and teachers, the myth has become the reality and the paradigm in terms of which they work. Many individuals have been educated within this paradigm and simply operate under the submerged assumptions that a primary purpose of interpreting a classical text in political theory is to illuminate a segment of the tradition and that the tradition is the principal intellectual context for interpreting these works.

It is now commonplace to assume that what have come to be accepted as the classic texts actually are the product of a "great" and "ongoing conversation" or "dialogue" and that "they form a coherent, if many-sided, tradition of thought."[1] Whether they advocate its study or simply see it as the prescientific background of the contemporary study of politics, political scientists as well as historians of political theory feel perfectly secure in referring to "the great tradition of political theory, from the fourth century B.C. until the beginning of the nineteenth century A.D."[2] The idea of the "Great Dialogue," its beginning, and its end (or near end) has become a matter of academic folklore. What is being discussed is not taken to be merely an abstraction or a metaphor but a specific activity which began in Athens and which, while remaining rooted in the world of politics, gained considerable "self-consciousness" and "independence" from particular circumstances in its continuing consideration of the great issues.[3] It is maintained that "whatever else they have done, political theorists in the Western tradition have been conducting a dialogue with each other" and that the dialogue is the "vehicle" of this tradition of "systematic reflection on politics."[4]

The idea of political theory as a vocation is accepted quite literally in the textbook literature, as is the idea that "political theorists share some fundamental understanding about their form of inquiry that enables them to speak to one another across vast reaches of time, space, and political culture."[5] The sense of practical concern, with regard to both explaining the present and confronting contemporary political problems, is prominent. There is the presumption that the conventional chronology is tied together, and related to the present, by a kind of "seamlessness" which explains its "great influence upon the political climate and institutions existing today."[6] Textbooks that treat the classic works seriatim in successive chapters proclaim that they are presenting the "evolution of political ideas from Plato to the present" and that they are engaged in "a careful tracing of the thread of the tradition in political philosophy."[7] In reading a textbook on the history of political theory, we are led to assume that we are actually studying how we have "come by our own political ideas" and tracing their genealogy from the point of their "Miraculous Birth" in ancient Greece.[8] All this is the conceptual residue of the myth of the tradition.

The extent to which the idea of the tradition has been consciously employed by certain historians as a persuasive device to lend authority to a critique of modern politics varies considerably, but the myth of the tradition had its origins in these practical concerns. What may first appear as methodological difficulties in some works may in some instances be less important if the intentions of the historians are clearly understood. Before they are viewed too harshly as violators of the historical attitude, it is necessary to take a careful look at what they are in fact doing. I do not presume to undertake an intellectual biography of the individuals discussed in the last chapter. My purpose is to offer brief interpretative suggestions rather than to provide any complete exposition of their work. However I do wish to look more carefully at the use of the idea of the tradition in their arguments and to inquire in more detail into the precise character of their enterprises.

HISTORY AS RHETORIC

Strauss's vision of the tradition was to a large extent a direct response to the attack on this field of scholarship by contemporary political scientists, and to designate much of his work as historical, in any very literal sense, would be misleading and would distort the character of both his representations of the tradition and his exegetical work. To point to fallacies in his method would be of little aid in understanding his argument. His account of the tradition is intelligible only in view of the argument about contemporary politics and political ideas that it supports, and it is quite apparent that his interpretation of figures such as Locke is designed to impugn what is commonly accepted as the intellectual foundations of modern liberalism.

Although Strauss puts great emphasis on understanding authors as they understood themselves, this prescription remains largely an unexplicated maxim. Apart from a thesis about political philosophy as a literature characteristically written in the context of threats of persecution and his insistence on the need to look beyond exoteric arguments, or the philosophers' public speech, and apparent inconsistency for arcane doctrinal meaning,[9] Strauss has little to say about the criteria of interpretation. Nowhere does he set forth anything approaching a general theory of textual interpretation that would give substance to his demand for historical objectivity. Yet this claim regarding hidden meaning and special techniques of discovery functions, as do many aspects of his description of the tradition, to insulate the argument from critical discussion. To speak of political philosophy as a tradition begun by Socrates, transformed by Machiavelli, and atrophying in the modern age or to postulate a modern political crisis and characterize it in terms of a catalogue of isms which are to be explained by the evolution of other isms amounts to more evocation than demonstration.

Strauss's description of both the modern crisis and the intellectual forces that produced it lacks contact with concrete events and moves within a realm of discourse which not only defies criticism but conflicts with his demand for confronting ideas on their own terms. A conflation of politics and political ideas persists in his work, and political philosophers are sometimes treated as if they were legislators for an age and sometimes as if they were representatives of stages in the tradition. Precisely how individuals such as Machiavelli have effected the great impact on the thought and practice of Western society that Strauss attributes to them is never clarified, and the evidence that would give credence to the causal connections between ideas and actions to which he continually alludes is rarely even suggested.

Similar problems are apparent in Strauss's approach to interpreting particular works. Despite his insistence on understanding an author's actual intention, he ascribes to the authors he analyzes the general intention to engage in the activity of political philosophy, as Strauss defines that activity, and already counts them as participants in the alleged tradition. The particular intention attributed to an author (such as Machiavelli's intention to transform classical political philosophy) is principally a function of the place that Strauss assigns him in the reconstructed tradition rather than something clearly elicited from the author's work. Although Strauss enjoins the reader to avoid all preconceptions and move entirely within the "circle of ideas" of the author himself,[10] he systematically avoids any such program and must avoid it, given his preconceptions about the existence and character of the tradition as well as his instrumental concerns in approaching it. The works which Strauss selects for the tradition are already meaningful within his vision of the tradition before he sets about interpreting them.

There is good reason to believe that in Strauss's case the myth of the tradition is quite consciously employed as a rhetorical device. Otherwise, it would indeed be difficult to account for the fact that his rendition of the course of the tradition and the development of modern political thought seems to reflect elements of the very historicism that he so vehemently repudiates. Once pieced together, his story of the decline of the West embodies a rather extravagant symbolism. Although he stresses a separation of philosophy and history and a distinction between interpretation and evaluation, he employs an approach in which a philosophical argument about politics is entirely dependent upon a historical account and in which interpretations of past thinkers are absolutely inseparable from his critique of contemporary politics. His condemnation of modernity involves an invocation of its origins and the revelation of a truth that lies buried beneath the dross of the tradition. His assertion that historical investigation is merely a preliminary undertaking required in order to recover the true character of political philosophy and to achieve an unadulterated perception of political phenomena and values is difficult to accept when nearly the entire body of Strauss's scholarship consists of this type of investigation.

One might suggest that Strauss is simply unable to extricate himself from the very intellectual tendencies he abhors, but it may be more reasonable to assume that he employs a historical argument because he believes himself compelled to do so in an age in which only historical arguments and historical symbolism carry meaning and authority. It requires very little effort to expose the methodological difficulties that arise if Strauss's work is taken as a straightforward exercise in the history of ideas, but it is necessary to point out that many of the commentaries on the history of political theory have become a kind of political theory which itself requires interpretation. Particularly, it is necessary to clarify how the drama of the tradition created by this literature provides a field of action for the therapeutically inclined historian.

Since the modern crisis is, in Strauss's view, largely a result of historical thinking, Strauss suggests that there is "no more appropriate way of combating this teaching than the study of history" and the employment of a "historical form" of critique.[11] In one place, Strauss argues that "only because public speech demands a mixture of seriousness and playfulness, can a true Platonist present the serious teaching, the philosophical teaching, in a historical and hence, playful garb."[12] In Strauss's case, it may well be that the story of the tradition is a correlate to a philosophical argument or a surrogate when discursive argument is inadequate in much the same sense that Plato employs mythohistorical tales in his dialogues. The three waves in Strauss's account of the decline of the tradition also recall, and form a counterpoint to, the three waves in the construction of the philosopher's city in Plato's *Republic*. From another perspective, what Strauss is about may be likened to what Aristophanes is doing in his play the *Frogs* when lamenting the passing of tragedy and its role as the educator of society. Just as Aristophanes brings Aeschylus from the underworld to do battle with Euripides in a dramatic confrontation between the old and new teachers of the polis, Strauss descends into history to resurrect the ancients and confront the moderns. In both cases, the moderns, in the existential world, have won the day. In the realm of the drama, the old teachings are vindicated and modernity is subdued.

HISTORY AS PHILOSOPHY

Voegelin places less emphasis on the specific concept of the tradition as an evolving entity than the other writers considered here, and, in his later work, he even tends to depreciate the extent to which forms of political symbolization are intelligible as a "historical succession" or a historical " 'course.' "[13] He holds that the complexity of symbols generated in the past is too great to reduce to a series of stages, that "the process of history and such order as can be discerned in it, is not a story to be told from the beginning to its happy, or unhappy, end," and that the modern form of the philosophy of history "is definitely not a story of meaningful events to be arranged on a time line."[14] Significant aspects of meaning in history do not develop linearly, and the problem of interpretation is to recover the meaning of various "theophanic events" that have occurred in the "Metaxy" or "man's existence in the divine-human In-Between" where the truth of order is revealed.[15] The interpretation of history involves a "movement through a web of meaning with a plurality of modal points,"[16] and the ideas that the historian encounters are somewhat epiphenomenal products of the unfolding experiences which arise from a search for the truth of order in society and for the place of society in the order of being.

Yet even if this, to some degree, is a break with his original project, Voegelin does not depart significantly from his substantive reconstruction of the course of Western civilization and the crisis of the modern age. He still believes that it is possible to perceive "dominant lines of meaning" in the history of political symbols such as the movement from compactness to differentiation and the progressive deformation of symbols in the modern age. Although he may not emphasize the concept of the tradition, the principal features of his work correspond to the basic characteristics of the myth of the tradition.

If Strauss utilizes something similar to the philosophy of history as a rhetorical strategy, Voegelin, despite his strong rejection of the substance of the philosophies of history of the eighteenth and nineteenth centuries, sees such philosophy as a uniquely "Western symbolization" and self-consciously engages in this mode of analysis.[17] Voegelin's serious concern with this enterprise leads him to expound in considerable detail a formal theory of symbolic forms and symbolic transformation which makes it possible to engage him on the question of historical interpretation in a way that is not possible in the case of Strauss. At the same time, Voegelin's concern with the philosophy of history makes him vulnerable to the criticism that has largely rendered this type of speculation obsolete. The idea that the course of history constitutes an intrinsically meaningful order of events that is objectively discernible would require a more elaborate defense than that provided by Voegelin.

Voegelin quite literally presses such notions as the idea that certain thinkers are representative of the mind of an age or a stage in the evolution of human consciousness; that modern totalitarian political movements, as well as Western liberalism, are merely the pragmatic counterparts of an intellectual nihilism whose development can be discerned in the historical process; that historical study reveals something on the order of a transcendent truth of politics; that the entire scope of Western history can be viewed as an intelligible order; and that the present age is uniquely situated to perceive this order. The difficulty is that arguments of this sort are quite outside any context in which a meaningful discussion can take place unless one subscribes to this general vision of history. There are simply no criteria for evaluating such assertions, and in the end we are left much in the same dilemma as we are in the case of Strauss, that is, their validity becomes a matter of their rhetorical force.

There is no doubt that some of Voegelin's studies of the classic texts are creative and profoundly scholarly analyses. Nevertheless, despite the fact that they can to some degree be read fruitfully outside the context of his total project, they are often considerably vitiated by their subsumption within the general framework he imposes on the history of political theory. Thus, for example, just as Strauss suggests that Karl Marx must be understood as a Machiavellian, Voegelin maintains that "at the root of the Marxian idea we find the spiritual disease of the gnostic revolt."[18] Such an approach makes it quite impossible to raise serious questions about an adequate interpretation of Marx's work. For someone who has so explicitly opposed the end to rational discussion created by the categorization of arguments in terms of preconceived import, Voegelin's rendering of the ideas of various theorists in terms of his array of isms is somewhat surprising.

HISTORY AS ART

Although Arendt develops a specific theory of politics more fully than some of the other writers, she is probably less expansive about the character of the enterprise in which she is engaged. Neither the use of the tradition as a rhetorical device nor the philosophy of history are adequate models for understanding her work, although something of both approaches may be present in her account of the tradition. The concept of the tradition that forms the basis of her arguments may be best described as a kind of literary metaphor.

For Arendt the crisis of the modern age, that is the loss of a distinctly public realm and the demise of classical politics, is not a matter to which theory can respond with definite practical answers or prescriptions, but it does occasion a "reconsideration of the human condition from the vantage point of our newest experiences and our most recent fears."[19] She designates her effort as a series of exercises in thought and as an attempt "to think what we are doing" in the present, and the "only aim is to gain experience in *how* to think" in this situation.[20] Yet, at the same time, she points out that these "intervals" or thought-spaces in historical time created by the clash between past and future have "shown more than once that they may contain the moment of truth."[21] What is crucial, however, is her belief that "all thought begins with remembrance."[22] The past unavoidably pushes us forward into the future, but our concern, and the concern of every generation, is with "the future which drives us back into the past."[23] This is to be an "experimental" as well as "critical interpretation of the past," and the future is the concern which instigates the venture.[24]

It is easy to come away from Arendt's work with the impression that one has encountered a playful manipulation of the past and a free reconstruction of traditional concepts in light of present concerns. Historical events and ideas seem to have been interwoven into a great dramatic fabric which provokes insights, yet ultimately defies any critical analysis. There is much to suggest that something of this sort is close to her intention. She states quite clearly that she does not attempt to "be literally true to the sequence of theories and attitudes" but rather seeks to offer "a metaphorical approximation to what actually happened in the minds of men."[25] If taken as "history" in any strict sense, the connections she makes between the past and the present, and between ideas and events, would appear as little more than a series of spurious allusions.

She is explicit about her intention to "transform a historical figure into a model and assign to it a definite representational function,"[26] and only in these terms can we adequately grasp her nostalgic, idealized treatment of Greek politics and her characterization of such individuals as Plato and Marx. Yet it would be going too far to suggest that for Arendt the past is merely a medium to be manipulated at will. What she constructs from the past, in fact her total vision of the tradition, is an ideal type that is not, in her view, simply an instrumental fiction but the elaboration of something that "possessed a representative significance in reality which only needed some purification in order to reveal its full meaning."[27] It would be a mistake to assume that she does not believe that these exercises in the interpretation of historical concepts penetrate an "underlying phenomenal reality."[28]

I would suggest that although the kind of enterprise in which she is engaged is to some extent intelligible on its own terms, it exemplifies a pattern that finds its most influential expression in the existentialist philosophy of Martin Heidegger. There are a number of instances where the direct influence of Heidegger is apparent in her work, such as the acknowledged parallel between her interpretation of Plato and Heidegger's analysis of Plato's idea of truth.[29] Yet the similarities go much deeper, not only with regard to substantive matters, such as a common emphasis on Descartes's thought as a crucial stage in the advent of modernity, but with regard to the general form of the analysis of the tradition.

Like Strauss and Voegelin, who view Heidegger as the personification of historicism, Arendt, although in part for somewhat different reasons, is critical of Heidegger and emphasizes her debt to the philosophy of Karl Jaspers. She argues that Heidegger's brand of philosophy involves an extreme egoism that ultimately destroys the possibility of meaningful communication and "being-with-others," and she quite clearly believes that Heidegger's attitudes and actions with regard to National Socialism in Germany were to some degree culpable.[30] Nevertheless, whether it is a matter of common intellectual background or some other affinity of thought, the work of Arendt (and possibly the structure of arguments such as those of Strauss and Voegelin) shows marked parallels with Heidegger's philosophical project despite the often negative attitude toward him. The similarities are significant enough to warrant a brief description of this project.[31]

For Heidegger, the condition of modern man is one of homelessness born from the break in tradition caused by the ascendency of modern science and the domination of technology in Western culture. The "inauthentic" individual, who is unreflectively absorbed in the banality of everyday concerns and lives from moment to moment, fails to appreciate the finitude of his existence and the extent to which he is thrown into an alien world that he did not create. Temporality is the basic dimension of human existence, and human beings must realize and interpret themselves in the present through choices projected toward the future and grounded in the possibilities of the past. The authentic individual lives in terms of conscious repetition and anticipation. Western society as a whole has fallen into inauthenticity and fails to see how the catastrophies of the modern age are the culmination of a decadent metaphysical tradition which must be surpassed by creatively remembering the past in order to make it present and to engage the future. Yet the modern crisis also provides the possibility of thinking outside the tradition and signals the appearance of a totally new era emerging from the corpse of Western metaphysics.

For Heidegger, the problems of modernity are rooted in what he terms the "forgetting" of Being, or the loss of a primordial experience of the world. This loss had its beginning in the origins of metaphysics in Greece and particularly in the transition from pre-Socratic thought, with its idea of truth as "unconcealedness" or "unveiledness," to Plato and his idea of truth as conformance with a metaphysical fixed order of reality. The forgetting of Being must be overcome by reawakening the Being question and by returning to that original notion of truth and understanding the extent to which all succeeding epochs grew out of it. We must regain the sense of how Being first revealed itself in language, which Heidegger designates as the "house" of Being, and how language has also lost its original meaning as the tradition developed. The beginning and the end of the tradition are decisive moments, and only when the loss of the experience with which the tradition began becomes total is it possible to recapture that beginning in its fullness.

Heidegger, then, undertakes to demonstrate how the tradition of metaphysics that began with Plato has run dry with Nietzsche and Marx and their inversions and reversals of the tradition. He emphasizes that what appears as a rejection of the tradition in their work was in fact a consummation that remained bound within the categories of the tradition and within the orbit of what it negated. Out of the death of the tradition comes a period when old questions, as well as old answers, lose their meaning, and the result is the nihilism of the modern age. In this situation, history becomes the important science. The destruction of the tradition and the surpassing of metaphysics involves a recalling of the past, a rethinking of the meaning of historical concepts in terms of our present problems, and a recovery of their original spirit which has been obscured by the tradition.

For Heidegger, it is quite clear that historical analysis is circular and that all interpretation is from the standpoint of our present concerns. Yet this is not a simple relativism or perspectivism which involves merely reading meaning into history. The interpretation of the tradition and its relation to our present condition is not simply to be judged by whether it is true or false but rather by the extent to which it produces a consistent explanation of the present and an illumination of the contemporary dilemma. Heidegger's destruction of the tradition is not a severing of our connection with the past or a repudiation of it but an appropriation and transformation that allows us, within the horizon of the present, to adapt the past to our encounter with the future.

The general character of this project, as well as its concrete execution, is reflected in the work of Arendt, and perhaps it is instructive in understanding the kind of enterprise undertaken by individuals such as Strauss and Voegelin and identifying the intellectual tradition in which they stand. In the case of Arendt, one need only substitute politics for Being and political theory for metaphysics to see the parallels. Heidegger's argument will also be relevant to the discussion of textual interpretation in Chapter IV.

HISTORY AS EDUCATION

Wolin's work presents a somewhat different set of problems. Although his principal concern at times is to defend traditional political theory from modern political science and its claim to scientific theory and although his statement of "political theory as a vocation" in many respects summed up and epitomized the two decades of this debate between behavioralism and the history of political theory, his version of the tradition is not simply the consequence of this controversy. Further, although he wishes to explore critically the philosophical basis of contemporary politics, the idea of the tradition does not, as in the case of Strauss, serve as a basically instrumental concept. Unlike Voegelin, Wolin is not offering anything which can be reasonably construed as a philosophy of history, despite the existence of a certain shadow of that form which is common to all these writers. Finally, although he is concerned with demonstrating the decline of a distinctly public realm and political consciousness in modern society, his work, as distinguished from that of Arendt, is not primarily an exercise in rethinking the past. Yet, ironically, Wolin's claim about the tradition may in many respects be the most vulnerable to the charge of lacking historicity. While to some degree one inevitably misses the point of the arguments of Strauss, Voegelin, and Arendt if they are interpreted and judged in terms of something like an Oakeshottian paradigm of the historical attitude, Wolin, despite his practical reasons for engaging in a study of the history of political theory, embraces the idea of the tradition quite literally:

Wolin maintains that despite changing configurations of politics, the political has persisted as an object of knowledge, and the history of political theory is the history of the tradition of inquiry directed towards that object. He maintains that "the idea of theory as a form of systematic knowledge systematically pursued" began in Greece and a "truly classical paradigm" emerged with the "classical synthesis" of politics, theory, and philosophy of Plato and Aristotle who "were the most influential in determining its methods and objectives for the next several centuries."[32] He believes that "political theory consists of very well-defined conventions relating to methods of inquiry, the constitution of the subject matter, and the purposes of inquiry" and that this mode of thought constitutes a vocation that can be traced historically and constitutes a tradition.[33] Wolin admits that "the notion of tradition presents difficult problems for the study of political theory,"[34] and he has attempted to explicate this concept in several ways.

He suggests that the history of political theory might be understood in terms of Thomas Kuhn's popular study of the structure of scientific revolutions and his theory of scientific change as a movement from one paradigmatic mode of scientific theory and practice to another. Classical political theorists would be the counterparts of Galileo and Newton or creators of master paradigms within which lesser thinkers have moved in conducting "normal" and cumulative political studies. He also suggests that it may be reasonable to think of political society itself as a paradigm of normal science and of the classic works as instances of extraordinary science or challenges to existing paradigms.[35] In many respects, this analogy may provide interesting insights into the character of certain classic works, but as an explanation of the tradition it has severe difficulties. First of all, there is the problem of demonstrating that there is in fact a significant similarity between the history of science and the history of political theory. There is a question whether the history of what is called political theory is in any way a history of disciplined activity comparable to that of science, and it is even more doubtful that the relationship of the classic theorist to politics is similar to that of the revolutionary scientist to the scientific community. The argument that the classic works have created followers in this sense is difficult to sustain, and there would seem to be more reason to suggest that the counterpart, for example, of Newton in politics might be someone such as Cromwell rather than Hobbes. Furthermore, the argument, if taken as more than a simile, tends to be regressive, since it entails the acceptance of Kuhn's controversial thesis about the history of science.[36]

In a somewhat related argument, Wolin has attempted to portray the tradition as a succession of "epic" or "heroic" theories which are to be understood as "an attempt to compel admiration and awe for the magnitude of their achievement."[37] He suggests "that from Plato to modern times an epic tradition in political theory has existed . . . which is inspired mainly by the hope of achieving a great and memorable deed through the medium of thought."[38] However, this argument hardly seems to solve the problem of the tradition as originally posed, that is, the idea of the tradition as a continuing dialogue over time which compels participants to conform to certain rules and modes of discourse.[39] The epic tradition is an extrapolation from a survey of "the acknowledged masters" which may offer some insight into "the intentions which prompted epical theories."[40] It is not a historically definable activity which provides the context for understanding particular works. It is an abstraction from particular works.

At the core of Wolin's claim, and at the core of the myth of the tradition, is the assumption that whatever the immediate problem the theorist concerned himself with, and no matter what the concrete circumstances of his thought, his participation in the tradition of political theory is the primary factor in interpretation, and this participation is also the source of the tradition. Wolin presents the vocation of creating political theory as a historical phenomenon, yet his work is not so much devoted to demonstrating the existence of the tradition as to commenting on its character and implications. He suggests that "testimony that such a vocation has existed is to be found in the ancient notion of the *bios theoretikos* as well as in the actual achievements of the long line of writers extending from Plato to Marx,"[41] but its historical status is ambiguous. The idea of the tradition as a distinct object of inquiry remains elusive.

TRADITION: HISTORICAL AND ANALYTICAL

In arguing that what is often accepted as *the* tradition is a myth, it is necessary to be precise about the nature of this claim and about what is not being claimed. First of all, I am not suggesting that there are no reasons for considering the classic works as classic, but I do maintain that it is not because they are part of a demonstrable historical tradition. It is often difficult to avoid the conclusion that what is referred to as the tradition is simply the canon of classic works and that these works are designated as classic because they are elements of the tradition. I do not wish to imply that there is no basis for viewing all the authors of these works as addressing themselves to a range of perennial problems of political life that transcend their most immediate concerns and historical circumstances. From various perspectives and at various levels of abstraction one could say that they all discussed such issues as justice, power, authority, obligation, and freedom. This is merely a matter of imposing analytical or topical categories and of describing them from a particular standpoint. Finally, it is not necessarily problematical to specify, on the basis of some criterion or other, certain similarities and differences in a range of chronologically ordered works and speak of this as a tradition with continuity and change. Although this may be a somewhat restricted and specialized, and even metaphorical, use of the term, it is certainly not an unusual application, especially in scholarly disciplines. It is probably in this sense that one refers to something such as the rationalist tradition in philosophy or traditional democratic theory. The problem is not one of discovering, or legislating, a proper definition of tradition but rather of making relevant distinctions and avoiding confusions between the uses of the term. One important distinction, particularly in the case of the history of political theory, is that between what might be termed analytical and historical traditions.

It may be very useful to locate a work in some thematic context and relate it to other works which, according to some criterion, fall within the same category. Oakeshott, for example, states that "the masterpiece of political philosophy has for its context, not only the history of political philosophy as the elucidation of the predicament and deliverance of mankind, but also, normally, a particular tradition in that history."[42] Yet this isolation of the history of political philosophy and the specification of subtraditions governed by such items as "reason and nature" or "will and artifice" are clearly analytical exercises and not references to historically discriminated patterns of persistence and change. In other words, the tradition distinguished here is a convention of scholarship and not a convention of the works themselves. I am not suggesting that there are simply historical givens which are apparent and indisputable. Any statement about a tradition, whether analytical or historical, is hypothetical and open to criticism regarding whether the tradition exists or, in the case of analytical tradition, whether there are grounds for viewing certain works as belonging. The problem is to prevent a confusion in reference.

To a large extent the development of the idea of the tradition was a consequence of the gradual reification of a category which originally merely distinguished analytically a particular body of literature and series of themes and problems. In other words, the idea of the tradition as a scholarly convention came to be conceived as a preexisting historical phenomenon, that is, as a historical tradition. This process was complemented, or completed, by a similar transformation regarding the activity of political theory. The notion of traditional political theory as a historical activity and disciplined mode of inquiry was essentially a matter of bestowing misplaced historical concreteness on what was originally an ideal typification composed of attributes derived from a survey of selected writers and thinkers. The works and theories of specific authors were in turn designated as instances or products of this activity. The appearance of the myth of the tradition was very much a matter of intellectual evolution, that is, the creation of a qualitatively new idea by temporalizing analytical differences and similarities and endowing the sequence with an elaborate intrinsic meaning and structure with causal import for understanding contemporary political thought and action.

It is not my intention to suggest that there are no actual historical connections between the works usually cited as belonging to the tradition. Yet if at the root of the myth of the tradition is the tendency to speak of an analytical tradition as if it were a historical tradition, the myth is also supported by the tendency to extrapolate spuriously from the existence of certain historical connections between these works and from the presence of certain actual historical traditions and schools of thought. There is no doubt that the authors of the classic works saw themselves as addressing issues of universal and timeless significance and that sometimes a similarity, and even a continuity, in the discussion of certain problems was recognized by the theorists themselves. There are certainly instances in which a theorist noted a similarity between his enterprise and that of a predecessor who has since been added to the Pantheon of political theory. Occasionally an author has specifically and overtly directed his argument toward a past thinker to either reject or draw upon the authority of that argument, and some have done so in a less explicit manner. In addition, there are various historical connections between these works and indications of varying degrees of the influence of one upon another. For example, Aristotle criticized as well as worked within the framework of Plato's arguments and the philosophy of the Socratic school; Roman writers such as Cicero consciously emulated the thought and style of Greek philosophy; there are numerous Hellenic themes in the work of Augustine; Aquinas relied heavily on Aristotle's political thought; Machiavelli alludes to various ancient authors including Plato, Aristotle, and Polybius; Hobbes translated Thucydides and concerned himself with the impact of Aristotle's ideas on the intellectual life of the seventeenth century; Locke probably had Hobbes in mind in several respects; Rousseau took pains to demonstrate his acquaintance with past political thinkers and adapted such symbols as the "social contract" utilized by Hobbes and Locke to his own argument; and Marx's incorporation, as well as transformation, of ideas associated with such thinkers as Hegel keeps many intellectual historians occupied.

Such numerous and generally recognized connections may be quite relevant in the interpretation of certain specific historical texts, but they may also be quite insignificant and become exaggerated if one assumes that an author's basic concern was to participate in the Great Dialogue. In any event, although such connections may lend force to the idea of the tradition, they in no way give substance either to the assumption of the existence of the tradition or to the principal claims about it. Individual classic texts may very well be part of some tradition in philosophy or other form of thought and either consciously or unconsciously participate in it. It is also probably innocuous to say that these works are all part of the Western political tradition, but this is little more than a truism. Sometimes it is relevant to locate a work within a school of thought such as in the case of John Stuart Mill and Utilitarianism, and it might not be straining the concept too much to refer to this as a tradition. However, to suggest that this is a subtradition within the great tradition is misleading, just as it would be to suggest that Mill could be said to belong to the great tradition and to assign him the motive of participating in that tradition in the same sense that he might be described as writing within the Utilitarian tradition.

Allowing for all the special uses that might be made of the concept of tradition, it is worth noting that usually the term refers to the transmission of ideas or modes of action through an inherited pattern of thought and practice associated with some fairly well-defined activity and realm of discourse. It implies a situation where knowledge, belief, or custom is handed down (often orally) through successive generations bound together in some common activity or form of social action. The term suggests a body of long-established and generally accepted and authoritative forms of thought and behavior.[43] It is quite clear that the literal and customary meaning of tradition little resembles its use in designating the corpus of works strung together to compose the history of political theory. There is no such context as *the* tradition into which the classic texts have been inserted, and the dramatic teleological structure supported by the idea of the tradition must be recognized as a myth. One of the features of much of the so-called traditional literature of political theory was its untraditional character, not only in the sense that it was innovative but in the sense that it was not integrally related to the political community but was marked by its alienation from it. These works were often outside traditional political thought and action and had little to do with their development. This literature certainly does not constitute a tradition of its own, although analytically one might find grounds for speaking of it in this way. The tradition was an invention of the historian. Yet the concept of tradition carries a force important for the persuasiveness of arguments associated with this myth. The unity of theory and practice and the interrelationship of ideas and action, as well as the relevance of the past for the present, which characteristically belong to the meaning of tradition are essential to the literature and its attempt to relate organically the classic texts to contemporary politics.

One can grasp an implicit motive of much of the literature of the myth of the tradition by understanding the extent to which it mirrors its own image of the activity of political theory. There is a rather general agreement among these commentators about the character of political theory. This includes viewing political theory as a response to a crisis, as a diagnosis of disorder and a critique of contemporary politics, as a search for the truth of political order and human nature, and as the construction of a vision of a new political society. Such characteristics are reflected in the historian's own work, but they appear as aspects of a historical interpretation. The historians view their enterprise as a practical response to a modern crisis and as a search for an explanation as well as a remedy. It is a historicized replication of political theory. In many respects, this kind of literature is a surrogate for political theory. It is an academic imitation of a particular view of classical literature, but it tends to lack the concrete and creative engagement with political problems that characterizes the original works. In this respect, Easton, Strauss, Cobban and others may be quite correct in recognizing, despite the somewhat different grounds of this recognition, that the history of political theory is not the same as political theory itself and that the decline of political theory is tied to its transformation into an academic discipline.

My concern, however, is not to denigrate this literature but rather to clarify the endeavor which has produced it and the assumptions that are involved and to suggest some of the difficulties that arise if the idea of the tradition is taken literally. I will attempt to demonstrate in the final chapter that there are, to be sure, family resemblances between what we take to be the classic works and there are similarities between the circumstances and concerns of the authors which justify comparison and generalization and even an attempt to isolate them retrospectively and analytically, consider them together as a type of literature, and discuss, from various perspectives, their relationship to contemporary thought and action. This is quite different, however, from suggesting that political theory has been a historically recognizable conventional activity into which the diverse writers normally considered as constituting the tradition of political theory have entered, and that their work is the core of an inherited pattern of thought which can be traced backward and causally related to contemporary politics. To subscribe to this view is to perpetuate a myth which often disables attempts to engage the problem of the criteria of textual interpretation and the explanation of conceptual change.

NOTES

1. Dante Germino, "The Contemporary Relevance of the Classics of Political Philosophy," in Fred I. Greenstein and Nelson W. Polsby, eds., *Handbook of Political Science,* vol. 1, *Political Science: Scope and Theory,* (Reading: Addison-Wesley, 1975), pp. 230, 235, 237; Thomas A. Spra-

gens, Jr., *Understanding Political Theory* (New York: St. Martins, 1976), p. 8; David Thomson, ed., *Political Ideas* (Baltimore: Penguin, 1969), p. 11.

2. Karl W. Deutsch and Leroy N. Rieselbach, "Recent Trends in Political Theory and Political Philosophy," *The Annals of the American Academy of Political and Social Science* 360 (July 1965): 143; Gerald Runkle, *A History of Western Political Theory* (New York: Ronald Press, 1968), p. v.

3. Dwight Waldo, "Political Science: Tradition, Discipline, Profession, Science, Enterprise," in Greenstein and Polsby, *Political Science,* p. 8.

4. Lee Cameron McDonald, *Western Political Theory* (Harcourt, Brace and World, 1968), pp. 4, 606.

5. Spragens, p. 8.

6. Mulford Q. Sibley, *Political Ideas and Ideologies: A History of Political Thought* (New York: Harper and Row, 1970), p. 5; M. Judd Harmon, *Political Thought: From Plato to the Present* (New York: McGraw-Hill, 1964), p. 1.

7. William Ebenstein, *Political Thought in Perspective* (New York: McGraw-Hill, 1957), p. ix; Charles N. R. McCoy, *The Structure of Political Thought* (New York: McGraw-Hill), p. 8; Henry J. Schmandt, *A History of Political Philosophy* (Milwaukee: Bruce Publishing Co., 1960), p. 8.

8. Christopher Morris, *Western Political Thought* (New York: Basic Books, 1967), pp. ix, 9.

9. Leo Strauss, *Persecution and the Art of Writing* (Glencoe, Ill.: Free Press, 1952).

10. Leo Strauss, *On Tyranny* (Glencoe, Ill.: Free Press, 1963), p. 25.

11. Ibid., p. 27.

12. Leo Strauss, "Farabi's Plato," in *Louis Ginsberg, Jubilee Volume* (New York: The Academy for Jewish Research, 1945), pp. 376–77.

13. Eric Voegelin, *Order and History,* vol. 4, *The Ecumenic Age* (Baton Rouge: Louisiana State University Press, 1974), pp. 1, 2.

14. Ibid., pp. 2, 57.

15. Ibid., p. 56.

16. Ibid., p. 57.

17. Eric Voegelin, *Order and History,* vol. 2, *The World of the Polis* (Baton Rouge: Louisiana State University Press, 1957), p. 23.

18. Leo Strauss, *What is Political Philosophy?* (Glencoe, Ill.: Free Press, 1959), p. 41. Eric Voegelin, *From Enlightenment to Revolution* (Durham: Duke University Press, 1975), p. 298.

19. Hannah Arendt, *The Human Condition* (New York: Doubleday, 1958), p. 6.

20. Ibid., p. 6; Hannah Arendt, *Between Past and Future* (New York: Viking, 1961), p. 14.

21. Arendt, *Between Past and Future,* p. 9.

22. Hannah Arendt, *On Revolution* (New York: Viking, 1963), p. 222.

23. Arendt, *Between Past and Future,* pp. 10–11.

24. Ibid., p. 15.

25. Ibid., p. 9.

26. Hannah Arendt, "Thinking and Moral Considerations," *Social Research* 38 (Autumn 1971): 427.

27. Ibid., p. 428.

28. Arendt, *Between Past and Future,* p. 15.

29. Ibid., p. 235.

30. Hannah Arendt, "What is Existenz Philosophy?" *Partisan Review* 13 (1946): 34–56, see esp. p. 46.

31. See, for example, Martin Heidegger, *What is Philosophy?* (New York: Twayne Publishers, 1958); *An Introduction to Metaphysics* (New Haven: Yale University Press, 1959); *Existence and Being* (Chicago: H. Regnery, 1949); *The End of Philosophy* (New York: Harper and Row, 1973).

32. Sheldon S. Wolin, "Political Theory: Trends and Goals," *International Encyclopedia of the Social Sciences,* vol. 12 (New York: Macmillan, 1968), pp. 318, 319.

33. Ibid., p. 319.

34. Sheldon S. Wolin, "Communications," *American Political Science Review* 64 (June 1970): 592.

35. Sheldon S. Wolin, "Paradigms and Political Theories," in Preston King and B. C. Parekh, eds., *Politics and Experience* (Cambridge: Cambridge University Press, 1968), pp. 139–41, 149, 151.

36. See Thomas Kuhn, *The Structure of Scientific Revolutions* (Chicago: University of Chicago Press, 1970).

37. Sheldon S. Wolin, *Hobbes and the Epic Tradition of Political Theory* (Los Angeles: William Andrews Clark Memorial Library, University of California, 1970), p. 5.

38. Ibid., p. 4.

39. Sheldon S. Wolin, *Politics and Vision* (Boston: Little, Brown, 1960), p. 22.

40. Ibid., p. 2; Wolin, *Hobbes and the Epic Tradition of Political Theory,* p. 10.

41. Sheldon S. Wolin, "Political Theory as a Vocation," *American Political Science Review,* 63 (December 1969), 1078.

42. Michael Oakeshott, "Introduction," Thomas Hobbes, *Leviathan* (Oxford: Blackswell, 1957), p. xii.

43. *The Oxford English Dictionary,* vol. XI (Oxford: Clarendon Press, 1933); *Webster's Third New International Dictionary* (Springfield, Ma.: Merriam, 1971).

Thomas Hobbes 1588–1679

IV

The Problem of Interpretation

Though words be the signs we have of one another's opinions and intentions; yet, because the equivocation of them is so frequent according to the diversity of contexture, and of the company wherewith they go . . . it must be extreme hard to find out the opinions and meaning of those men that are gone from us long ago, and have left us no other signification thereof but their books.

Hobbes

THE "NEW" HISTORY OF POLITICAL THEORY

It was inevitable that the literature that propagated, and participated in, the myth of the tradition would fall subject to an attack on the grounds that the arguments lacked historicity. This literature became the target of the historical attitude precisely because the arguments about the tradition were masquerading as historical theses. What some have come to view as the new history of political theory, or at least the proposal for undertaking a new type of historical analysis of political ideas, is to some extent the product of an increasing detachment from the practical concerns that had generated much of the previous literature. It involves an emphasis on methodological issues relating to the study of past political theory. However, although this emphasis may be a symptom of the decline of practical and critical concerns, it is also in some respects a heritage of the myth of the tradition. The problem of methodology had always been implicit, and often explicit, in the works of the prominent interpreters of the tradition. If the problem was to elicit wisdom from the past and separate error and falsehood, the question of how properly to undertake this task could hardly be avoided. It was an intrinsic aspect of claims about the tradition. Yet, since these were actually largely unhistorical arguments, the methodological discussions were seldom carried through in a satisfactory manner.

To some extent, the growth of methodological concerns must also be attributed to an attenuation of one of the central issues associated with the last phase in writing about the tradition, that is, the conflict between so-called scientific and traditional political theory. It was in part the myth of traditionalism incorporated in the behavioralist critique which had occasioned the myth of the tradition, but, by the late 1960s, the debate was winding down. The resolution of this conflict between the dominant persuasion in political science and the subfield of the history of political theory was not so much the elimination of either contestant as the retirement of each to his respective endeavor. Behavioralism in political science became more concerned with attacks on the integrity of its conception of the scientific enterprise and its particular assumptions about the nature of scientific explanation than with prosecuting the case for a science of politics against the claims of traditionalism. Similarly, the concerns of some historians of political theory began to turn inward as this controversy subsided, and it was inevitable that they would move closer to general problems associated with the history of ideas. Issues relating to the epistemology of history or the character of historical knowledge and how to recover the meaning of past texts gained greater significance. The study of political theory originated with practical concerns, but its fate was to become increasingly a purely scholarly endeavor bound to the issues of the symbolic form, in this case history, which was its principal mode of expression.

As I noted in Chapter I, the recent critique of scholarship in the history of political theory started from the bottom up, that is, from an analysis of the apparent methodological problems inherent in its specific claims about the past rather than from a consideration of exactly what these historians had been doing and what type of literature they produced. These problems were defined largely in terms of a general conception of the history of ideas and the issues relating to the recovery of historical meaning. There was a singular lack of analysis of the intentions and purposes of this literature, and, consequently, much of the criticism was pertinent only on the basis of the assumptions that this literature was in fact the product of the historical attitude, and that those being criticized had the same basic concerns as the critics. The attitude, however, was essentially practical. While the literature characteristic of the myth of the tradition tended to emphasize *what* should be studied and *why*, the historical critique concentrated on the problem of *how* and assumed that the former questions were distinct and ancillary issues. While, for those within the myth of the tradition, what works were chosen for inclusion and why they were studied were dictated by the concerns of the present, the critics wished to develop a method for excising the influence of present predispositions and for achieving an objective reconstruction of the meaning of past texts, and they insisted on a strict distinction between the historical meaning of a work and its subsequent influence and significance.

Although individuals such as Quentin Skinner argue that it is probably impossible for an interpreter to attain complete objectivity by eliminating all preconceptions, they maintain that the first goal of historical investigation must be to understand the meaning of the text through a recovery of the author's intentions and his understanding of his own situation, and that this requires, insofar as possible, a neutralization of the influence of the interpreter's present circumstances. Drawing examples from various works dealing with the history of political ideas, Skinner catalogues the range of fallacies in interpretation that, in his view, arise from a failure to recognize that the recovery of the meaning of texts "presupposes the grasp both of what they were intended to mean, and how this meaning was intended to be taken."[1] He charges that much of this literature has involved: anachronistic and unwarranted impositions of modern assumptions and categories of analysis on the data; the extremes of either seeking the author's meaning from an analysis of the text alone or attempting to view this meaning as simply an expression of a particular social context; a failure to distinguish an explanation of the production of a work from an understanding of what the author was saying; and other mistakes which in one way or another follow from an unhistorical attitude toward past ideas and events and from, in particular, not acknowledging the "special authority of an agent over his intentions" and the need to discover those intentions in order to understand the historical meaning of a work. For Skinner, the task of an interpreter of a text is to determine "what its author, in writing at the time he did write and for the audience he intended to address, could in practice have been intending to communicate," and "to recover this complex intention on the part of the author."[2] In Skinner's view, the study of the history of political thought requires a method for accomplishing this task. Skinner is not alone in defending this position, and he specifically acknowledges his debt to, and sympathy with, the arguments of John Dunn and J. G. A. Pocock.

Dunn, noting that studies in the history of political theory have been criticized sometimes for historical "falsity" and sometimes for philosophical "incompetence," argues that not only are both "historical specificity" and "philosophical delicacy" important but that they "are more likely to be attained if they are pursued together."[3] He maintains that "the connections between an adequate philosophical account of the notions held by an individual in the past and an accurate historical account of these notions is an intimate one."[4] Yet, although Dunn wishes to emphasize the complementarity of philosophical and historical analysis, his principal concern is to point to the unhistorical character of many of the studies in the history of political theory. Such histories, he argues, have often been histories of abstractions and fictions conjured up in the present and read back into the past rather than "any sort of historical account of an activity" actually existing in the past.[5] He insists that the thought of the past must be investigated as a social and linguistic activity if there is to be a truly historical understanding of it, since "one cannot know what a man means unless one knows what he is doing."[6] For Dunn, the history of political thought should be a history of descriptive and normative propositions and a history of the "activities in which men were engaged when they enunciated these propositions."[7] These propositions were stated by individuals who intended to say and do certain things by stating them. They were engaged in a particular kind of linguistic activity which was in turn part of a more general social or political activity. Thus to understand the thought of the past requires that we "return to the contexts of the utterances which men produce"; "the problem of interpretation is always the problem of closing the context" and historically locating the intentions and experiences of the speaker.[8] History, Dunn acknowledges, is always written in terms of current philosophical interests and perspectives, but any reasonable philosophical account or analysis of past thought presupposes an adequate historical understanding of it, and "its historicity is its sufficient and its sole legitimate immunity from our philosphical prejudices."[9]

Pocock attacks the unhistorical character of the selection and interpretations of major works from Plato to Marx by philosophically inclined commentators who have persistently defined these works as elements of a special philosophical tradition and analyzed them in philosophical terms rather than as part of a more general history of ideas. Pocock argues that "the intellectual similarities between these systems were supposed to constitute the continuities, the dissimilarities between them the processes of change, of a historical order; but the order had not been built up by the methods of the historian."[10] In most cases, the objects of study were not actually historical phenomena at all but rather creations of the philosopher and his present concerns, and thus it is impossible to relate them to actual historical events and understand them historically. Instead of simply approaching the classic texts as philosophy, Pocock argues for the development of a method for "treating the phenomena of political thought as historical phenomena and—since history is about things happening—even as historical events: as things happening in a context which defines the kind of events they were."[11]

For all these individuals, the historical phenomena in question are conceived as essentially linguistic, that is, instances of linguistic action. Although there may be particular pragmatic difficulties which arise from the inaccessibility of evidence for correctly understanding linguistic artifacts from the past, there is in principle, they argue, no difference between the recovery of the historical meaning of a text and the understanding of speech acts in the present. It is a matter of locating the writer's discourse in the context of a normative language system that was available to the author and then relating it to particular historical events. For Skinner, "a strictly historical approach to the study of political thought" is largely a retrospective social science which, by providing "a realistic picture of how political thinking in all its various forms was carried on in the past," would ultimately make it possible "to establish connections between the world of ideology and the world of political action."[12] The thesis is similar to a number of closely allied arguments in the philosophy of social science which suggest that social scientific explanation requires that social action be understood in terms of its meaning for the actor and that this meaning can be ascertained by viewing the action as part of a context of rules, conventions, and forms of social activity.[13] Skinner argues that historical understanding, like understanding speech in general, requires locating an utterance in a context which includes both strictly linguistic conventions and the wider range of social and intellectual conventions relevant to understanding the act of communication. He insists that "to understand a text must be to understand both the intention to be understood, and the intention that this intention should be understood, which the text itself as an extended act of communication must at least have embodied."[14] He concludes that "the appropriate methodology for the history of ideas must be concerned, first of all, to delineate the whole range of communication which could have been conventionally performed on the given occasion of the utterance of the given utterance, and, next, to trace the relation between the given utterance and this wider *linguistic* context as a means of decoding the actual intention of the given writer."[15]

In a similar argument, Pocock holds that the historical understanding of a text involves a reconstruction of the context of communication and the location of the text within that context. Like Skinner, he argues that the purposes and intentions of an author are accessible in this manner. Since "men think by communicating language systems" which constitute their "conceptual worlds," an "individual's thinking may now be viewed as a social event, an act of communication and of response within a paradigm system, and as a historical event, a moment in a process of transformation of that system and of the interacting worlds which both system and act help to constitute and are constituted by."[16] Pocock draws heavily upon Thomas Kuhn's popular theory of paradigms and paradigm change in the history of science. Just as the theories and disciplinary matrix of a science constitute the meaning context of scientific statements, the relevant context for understanding the thought and language of the political thinker is the "political community," its "public language," and the complex of paradigms of which it is composed.[17] Pocock maintains that, methodologically, "the historian's first problem, then, is to identify the 'language' or 'vocabulary' with and within which the author operated, and to show how it functioned paradigmatically to prescribe what he might say and how he might say it."[18] In this way, it is possible to determine what an author could in principle have said and then narrow the focus to arrive at an understanding of what he intended to say, what he succeeded in communicating, how it was taken, and the effect that it had. Such claims about meaning amount to "hypotheses" which must be subjected to "verification" by "methods which are rigorously historical" and "tested by the rules of historical evidence."[19]

Although both Skinner and Pocock claim to be advocating a method for interpretation, what they present is not so much a method at all but rather a philosophical argument about interpretation. I will return to this point in the last section of this chapter, but labelling arguments unhistorical which they judge do not conform to their model of interpretation amounts to the same thing as designating explanations in some activity as unscientific that do not conform to a particular philosophical model of scientific explanation. What they specify as a method of interpretation is actually a claim about what they believe takes place, or should take place, in performing interpretations. Even if such accounts of interpretation were taken as correct in providing either an accurate description or a sound recommendation, they would not constitute a method for pursuing particular interpretations.

Skinner and Pocock undertake a critique of the existing scholarship in the history of political theory, but they do so in terms of a particular model of historical interpretation which they suggest as an explanation of, and a prescription for, successful understanding of past ideas. However, they neither fully explicate this model nor defend it against alternative models. Their thesis, particularly Skinner's, has been the subject of considerable critical comment,[20] but these commentaries have often accepted the authors' own definition of their project and have treated the thesis as a methodological proposal. The critics have focused on such issues as the internal logic of the argument, the difficulties in carrying out its mandates, and the restrictiveness of the approach it recommends. I am not concerned here with a critical analysis of their argument as a method but rather with examining it as a general philosophical claim about the nature of interpretation. It is as futile to criticize their method as a procedural guide to historical interpretation as it is for them to advance it as such a guide. What is at stake is not so much a matter of determining a procedure for interpreting historical texts as it is a question of what constitutes historical interpretation. The problem that the type of argument advanced by Skinner and Pocock presents is not so much one of whether their method can be effectively employed as whether they provide an adequate account of historicity. The position represents one side of a long-standing debate in the philosophy of interpretation or hermeneutics.

THE SEARCH FOR THE AUTHOR

In recent years, this argument has been most explicitly articulated and defended by Eric Hirsch.[21] Hirsch insists that the author is "the determiner of his text's meaning" and that it is necessary to resist relativist or historicist assumptions that would equate the meaning of a text with its significance for a particular interpreter and lead to the "banishment of the author."[22] He maintains that any reasonable and defensible interpretation must rest on the assumption that the meaning of a text is dependent on what the author intended to say and that, at least in principle, this meaning is "accessible," "determinate," "changeless," and "reproducible."[23] Temporal distance, Hirsch argues, is in principle of no particular consequence, although the further a work is from the contemporary world of the intrepreter, the more difficult it may be to recover and establish evidence for the meaning. For Hirsch, understanding a text is reconstructing the author's meaning, and this is a "re-cognitive" act that is based on the fact that the meaning is expressed in publicly shared rules, conventions, or types of language and literary genres which give it an objective status and make recovery possible. Language provides a range of possibilities in which the author's meaning can be uttered. Understanding begins with isolating the "intrinsic genre" of the work, that is, the author's choice of expressive form, as a primary context for locating meaning and then continues by reconstructing the meanings of the particular utterances that make up the text.[24] The determinacy of meaning makes knowledge in interpretation possible.

Hirsch rejects what he believes to be the skeptical claim of relativists and "cognitive atheists" who maintain that we necessarily always understand the meaning of a text in our own terms and from our own perspective. Although there may be no indefeasible and final determination of meaning, anymore than there is final truth in science, he maintains that it is possible, despite pragmatic difficulties, to master the linguistic context of a work and, as in any discipline, arrive at reasonable hypotheses or guesses which are more or less probable, depending on the extent to which they can stand up to logical criticism, evidential testing, and the challenge of alternative hypotheses. For Hirsch, significance is a function of viewing meaning from the perspective of an external context or framework. It is variable and subjective while meaning is objective and permanent. It is the difference between knowledge and value.[25] Evaluation, criticism, and discussions of historical significance are operations that are analytically separate from, and subsequent to, the determination or understanding of an author's meaning, and it is this meaning which is the primary standard for judging the validity of an interpretation. Unlike Skinner and Pocock, Hirsch is quite clear about the fact that he is advancing a theory of interpretation, and he is quite aware of the principal opposing hermeneutical theory which has, in recent years, been most extensively elaborated by H-G. Gadamer. Gadamer sets himself squarely against this mode of defining the problem as well as the solution to it, but the idea of understanding as recovering a *mens auctoris* has a long tradition. In order to comprehend the current controversy over historicity, it is necessary to grasp some of the arguments associated with individuals such as Schleiermacher and Dilthey. Hirsch places himself in this tradition.[26]

Hermeneutics, the study of the principles of interpretation, originated as part of a search for an art or technique for understanding biblical scripture and classical literature and for retrieving the original meaning of authoritative texts. The focus of concern was on gaps in understanding that arose in particular instances. It was the German theologian and philosopher Frederich Schleiermacher (1768–1834) who first approached hermeneutics as an epistemological problem, and his work marked the appearance of a definite conception of textual exegesis.[27] He posed the problem as one of how to avoid misunderstanding. Misunderstanding arises naturally, he suggested, because of the inevitable distance between the worlds of the author and the interpreter, and this distance must be overcome in a disciplined manner through the employment of a method which will reveal the author's meaning. The task, according to Schleiermacher, was to penetrate the subjectivity expressed in a text, and, in principle, this was the same as understanding speech. It involved understanding both the language in which the author expressed himself and the particular message that the author expressed in that language. The latter was Schleiermacher's principal concern, since it was necessary to go beyond what, on the surface, the text seemed to say, in light of the interpreter's understanding of the language, in order to reach the original meaning the author intended. Meaning was a function of the linguistic context of the author and his audience. For Schleiermacher, the recovery of an author's meaning was a somewhat "divinatory" activity which involved getting inside the mind of the author and reconstructing or reproducing his particular thoughts from a study of the linguistic artifacts. He viewed interpretation as a creative or artistic act which was ultimately possible because the author and the interpreter shared certain universal forms of life experience. Schleiermacher held that in some respects it was possible to understand an author better than he understood himself, since, in the reflective and reproductive act of interpretation, the context of the author's meaning was often brought to a level of consciousness that was not possessed by the author.

Wilhelm Dilthey (1833–1911) attempted to expand hermeneutical theory into a philosophy of historical knowledge and the human sciences in general that would justify these disciplines as methodologically distinct from, yet comparable to, the natural sciences.[28] He argued that, unlike naturalistic explanation, historical understanding, as well as all explanation of human activity, was basically psychological or intuitive. Such explanation was possible because of a fundamental identity of subject and object. Following Vico, he maintained that there was a special access to historical facts which made historical knowledge possible and at least as certain as knowledge of the natural world. Individuals made history through their actions, and both the historical actor and the historian were historical beings participating in the same life world. The continuity of life, expressed in individual actions which at the same time constituted and took place within cultural forms, was the key to understanding. Life, in its dynamic movement, was continually externalized or expressed in symbols, events, and institutions, and it could be understood or reproduced from a study of these words and signs. Historical understanding was not the explanation of alien objects but rather the apprehension of the intentional acts of a psyche that participated in the same stream of life as the interpreter.

Once Hegelian notions of final meaning in history and absolute historical knowledge had been abandoned and yet the idea of human consciousness as historical had been accepted, the basic dilemma which Dilthey faced was how claims to knowledge, comparable to those of the natural sciences, were possible in view of the fact that every interpreter was situated in a particular social and historical situation that determined his view of the world. Although consciousness might objectify itself in social structures and texts and although the basic continuity of life created the possibility of empathetic recovery, how in the end could the interpreter escape the limits of his historical horizon? Dilthey's answer was primarily an exhortation to develop a historical consciousness, a sense of the past that would allow the interpreter to transcend his own circumstances. Both this idea of a special historical consciousness as well as the notion that historical interpretation involves a recovery of the subjectivity of an author were further developed by R. G. Collingwood (1889–1943). Some of the current, and particularly the Anglo-American, versions of the thesis of interpretation as reconstruction of the author's intention and meaning can be linked more directly to Collingwood than to Dilthey, and his arguments have certain parallels with recent work in the philosophy of social science which equates the explanation of social action with understanding its meaning for the actor.

Collingwood viewed his analysis of historical knowledge as "thought of the second degree" or a philosophical reflection on historical thinking and the objects of historical thought. "How do historians know?" What is it about historical phenomena "that makes it possible for historians to know them?"[29] For Collingwood, the objects of historical investigation are the purposive "actions of human beings that have been done in the past," but, since unlike actions in the present they are not directly accessible to empirical observation, they must be apprehended by the interpretation of evidence in the form of documents.[30] Furthermore, this procedure is autonomous and cannot be illuminated in terms of an analogy with the natural sciences. It involves an understanding of the inside of historical actions which is a matter of "getting inside other people's heads" and "looking at the situation through their own eyes."[31] Thus, he concluded, "all history is the history of thought."[32]

Collingwood agreed with Dilthey that historical knowledge involved a reappropriation of past thought, but he believed that Dilthey had mistakenly assumed this to be a form of psychological analysis which aimed at the recovery of immediate experiences and which was still conceived too much in terms of a model of naturalistic explanation. For Collingwood, historical knowledge was to be gained by a rethinking of past thoughts which had been "expressed in language or other activity."[33] Such knowledge involved a "re-enactment of past thought in the historian's own mind" where these thoughts could be objectively known by being subjectively lived.[34] In this sense, it became a kind of introspection or self-knowledge to be achieved by active, critical, reflective thinking. Collingwood believed, like Dilthey, that in the sciences of human action there was a fundamental unity of subject and object that did not exist in the natural sciences and that this made possible a "knowledge of what mind has done in the past" by a "redoing" or "perpetuation" of this in the present.[35] Temporal distance, he argued, presented no particular problem, because what was reappropriated was not some particular transient state of consciousness but an "eternal" object, "the very same thought," which stands outside the flow of time. This recovery of past thought is an inferential activity whereby the historian, confronted with evidence from the past, imagines himself in the situation of the author and literally rethinks the questions before the author and reexperiences the author's situation. Collingwood even suggested that a designation of any period of the past as unintelligible was not so much the result of any characteristic of the period itself but a reflection of the inability of the particular historian to rethink that portion of the past. The historian "must be the right man to study that object," and "if for any reason he is such a kind of man that he cannot do this, he had better leave the problem alone."[36]

To know what happened in the past, Collingwood argued, is not a matter of memory or consulting authorities but a process of comparing claims about the past with our own experiences of what does or does not happen.[37] However it is more than a critical or analytical endeavor. It is essentially an interpolative or constructive activity which involves the "historical imagination." This imagination is an a priori faculty, "an original and fundamental activity of the human mind," like the imagination of the artist or the novelist. The only difference is that the historian's claims are meant to be true and must stand up to tests of internal consistency and evidence.[38] Collingwood believed that while scientific history may have occurred in the past, it was only in the modern age "that the methods of history have been revolutionized" and that such history has become "a thing within the compass of everyone."[39] He believed that in the present "historical thought has worked out a technique of its own, no less definite in its character and certain in its results than its elder sister, the technique of natural science."[40]

Historical thinking does not have an end any more than does the search for knowledge in natural science. The historical imagination is continually given new content as the past is reconstructed from the standpoint of the present. In this sense, the knowledge of the past is a regulative ideal which can never be fully realized, and "every new generation must rewrite history in its own way."[41] Historical knowledge, like scientific knowledge, has its own history.

Although it would be incorrect to suggest that Dilthey and Collingwood were attempting to present a method, in the sense of a technique, for interpretation, they were addressing a methodological issue, that is, discussing and analyzing what they believed to be the principles of inquiry in historical investigation. They were concerned with the epistemological problem of how knowledge of the past, and the meaning of texts, was possible and with the logical problem of justifying claims to knowledge in the human sciences. These problems were generally posed in terms of a comparison with natural science and of the question of how knowledge of human action could be a separate but equal form of knowledge. This question appeared particularly pressing because of what was assumed to be the principal object of knowledge, that is, the intentions, thoughts, or psychic experiences of authors and historical actors that were expressed in language and action and that did not seem to possess the objective character that distinguished the facts of natural science. Furthermore, the methodological cast of many of these arguments was a consequence of a confrontation with the dilemma of historicism or the problem of how an interpreter or historian could transcend the influence of his own subjectivity and historical circumstances and gain an adequate understanding of the past and the actual meaning of historical texts rather than merely assess their significance from the perspective of the present.

It is this range of problems that has persisted or been revived in the recent concern with historicity in interpreting the classic texts of political theory. For those who contend that interpretation involves a recovery of an author's intended meaning, the notion that intentions are externalized in certain forms of linguistic action seemed to provide a way for òvercoming the nagging problem of the distance (psychological, temporal, cultural) between the author and the interpreter and to suggest a "method" that was largely based on a reconstruction of what goes on in translating a language or understanding speech. It also seemed to offer a basis for the practice of historical science, as well as the human sciences in general, in that it recognized the intentional or mentalistic character of historical and social phenomena but at the same time promised that they could be studied objectively. What has been neglected in this recent literature, however, is a number of arguments which attempt to solve these traditional problems of historical knowledge by a rejection of the framework within which they were posed and by a fundamental redefinition of historical understanding. Such an alternative has been most systematically presented in the philosophical hermeneutics of H-G. Gadamer.

THE AUTONOMY OF THE TEXT

Gadamer insists that his purpose is not to develop a method of interpretation. He maintains, in fact, that the concern of traditional hermeneutical theory with the problem of method has obscured the character of the human sciences and the nature of human understanding in general by assuming that the objects of the human sciences can be approached in a way similar to the data studied by the natural sciences. This emphasis on method as a means of overcoming the subjectivity of the interpreter and objectively recovering the subjectivity of the author has, in Gadamer's view, distorted what actually happens in the course of understanding a text. He wishes to penetrate beyond the self-understanding of the human sciences which, he believes, has been distorted by their encounter with the philosophy of positivism and its definition of scientific method and objectivity. He insists that it is not possible to "simply accept the human sciences' own account of themselves" which is largely a derivation from philosophical analyses that have focused on viewing them from the perspective of the methods of natural science and have obscured "what their mode of understanding in truth is."[42] He wishes to demonstrate what the human sciences are and what, by the very nature of their enterprise, they must be rather than attempt either to produce "an art or technique of understanding" and "make prescriptions" for these sciences or to specify how they "must change in order to become philosophically legitimate."[43] Gadamer does not wish to condemn or proscribe a concern with method in the practice of the human sciences but only to suggest that certain formulations of method, within both the human sciences and philosophy, perpetuate an incorrect view of what constitutes understanding and how it is possible. For Gadamer, the problem of the universal or ontological conditions of human understanding must precede epistemological issues and the methodological concerns of particular disciplines.

Gadamer has two principal contentions. First, he rejects the idea that adequate understanding requires some sort of elimination of the influence of the circumstances of the interpreter. Second, he insists that in understanding a text, "the mens auctoris is not admissible as a yardstick."[44]

While earlier hermeneutical theory, influenced by Cartesian rationalism and Enlightenment ideals of knowledge, viewed the present situation of the knower as a constraint that must be overcome, Gadamer maintains that it is not only a necessary condition of all understanding but positively productive of understanding. To free one's self from the horizon of the present is no more possible than to free one's self from language, since "the experience of the world in language is 'absolute' " and "whoever has language 'has' the world."[45] For Gadamer, there is a fundamental unity of thought, language, and world. Human relations as well as the relationship of man to the world are linguistic and disclosed in language. Language is not to be taken primarily as an instrument for expressing subjectivity. "Language is not just one of man's possessions in the world, but on it depends the fact that man has a world at all."[46] This means that it does not make sense to speak of being imprisoned within language, since the very universality of language is what overcomes the particular relativities of language. "Understanding is language bound. But this assertion does not lead us into any kind of linguistic relativism." To learn a new language is only possible because one already knows a language, and thus there is "no captivity within a language."[47] Similarly, the particular cultural and historical horizon of an interpreter is not something that inhibits understanding but rather is the very basis of understanding.

Gadamer maintains that the narrow meaning and pejorative connotation that the Enlightenment theories of knowledge attached to the concept of prejudice were a mistake. Although our prejudices may at times be barriers to understanding, one "is not able to separate in advance the productive prejudices that make understanding possible from the prejudices that hinder understanding." Our prejudices "constitute the initial directiveness of our whole ability to experience," and "only the support of familiar and common understanding makes possible the venture into the alien."[48] Although an interpreter must be aware of his prejudices and the conditions of his historical situation, they are not subjective distortions to be exorcized by adherence to a method but rather the very foundation of knowledge. Our present historical horizon is the ground of understanding and the means of opening up the past. To exist within a historical horizon is an ontological condition, that is, a primordial situation of human being, and not an epistemological problem. Although there are regional, or particular disciplinary, problems of understanding, Gadamer, following Heidegger, stresses the universality of hermeneutics in the sense that "understanding is the original character of the being of human life itself."[49] Human being is historical, and the condition in which one finds oneself when trying to interpret the past or a text is merely the human condition writ small. For Gadamer, "we study history only insofar as we are ourselves 'historical' " and belong to a tradition that is "an effective moment of one's own being."[50] The notion of "effective history" is an essential aspect of Gadamer's analysis.

He maintains that "true historical thinking must take account of its own historicality."[51] While for those who were caught up in the problem of historicism, such reflection tended to lead either to relativism and skepticism or to an attempt to nullify or mitigate the influences of the interpreter's perspective, Gadamer wishes to demonstrate that "to understand within a tradition does not limit the freedom of knowledge but makes it possible."[52] Tradition mediates between the interpreter's horizon and the horizon of the past, and, no matter how we may characterize it, understanding "is always the fusion of these horizons which we imagine to exist by themselves."[53] From this perspective, "time is no longer primarily a gulf to be bridged" but the continuous ground of custom and tradition in which the present is rooted and in terms of which the past presents itself.[54] Temporal distance is productive since it both filters out error and provides new vantage points for eliciting meaning. The horizon of the present, which is the "effect" of history, is the condition of understanding and determines the selection of problems for investigation. By relating a text to one's own situation, understanding takes place. Gadamer maintains that "in view of the finite nature of our historical existence there is . . . something absurd about the whole idea of a uniquely correct interpretation."[55]

This leads to Gadamer's second, and most controversial, contention which is his thesis that the meaning of a text is never reducible to an author's intention and the context in which he wrote, and the meaning of an historical event is never reducible to the intentions of the actors. He argues that to search for such a core of meaning "is a pointless undertaking in view of the historicity of our being," and a "hermeneutics that regarded understanding as the reconstruction of the original would be no more than the recovery of dead meaning."[56] Although interpretation is in some sense a re-creation, it is not a replication of a past act but a reconstruction of meaning that is produced by a particular interpreter's encounter with a text. Like the interpretation of the performance of a musical score, "every repetition is equally an original of the work."[57] For Gadamer, "understanding means, primarily, to understand the content of what is said and only secondarily to isolate and understand another's meaning as such."[58] Gadamer maintains that "not occasionally only, but always, the meaning of a text goes beyond its author,"

> since every age has to understand a transmitted text in its own way, for the text is part of the whole of the tradition in which the

age takes an objective interest and in which it seeks to understand itself. The real meaning of a text, as it speaks to the interpreter, does not depend on the contingency of the author and whom he originally wrote for. It is partly determined also by the historical situation of the interpreter and hence by the totality of the objective course of history.[59]

What then, for Gadamer, is understanding and how does it take place? Central to his position is the Heideggerian idea that Being and the world are disclosed in language and that this disclosure transcends any particular author's intentions or purpose. Consequently, the concern of the interpreter should not be with what some individual may have thought but with what is said as it appears or presents itself to the reader. There can be no final or "correct" interpretation, because the interpretive horizon stands in the moving tradition of history. What a text says must be taken seriously, and the interpreter must enter into a conversation with the text and the perspective or horizon that is disclosed there. Interpretation arises out of a confrontation and resolution of horizons, that of the text and that of the interpreter, and the emergence of a common meaning established through the bridge of the tradition and a concern with a common subject matter. Interpretation is required when there is a breach or disturbance in communication and an alienation of meaning, and this gap is closed through a dialogue or dialectical encounter between past and present. Sometimes Gadamer speaks of interpretation as a process of question and answer, but maybe his most important analogy is that of a game. Interpretation is a matter of entering into an activity, and this involves being "played" by the activity more than the performance of any deliberate set of moves. He also likens understanding a text to being "grasped" by a work of art.

The point is that "what is fixed in writing has detached itself from the contingency of its origin and its author and made itself free for new relationships."[60] Tradition builds on the excess of meaning that goes beyond the intention of the author. Gadamer argues that to interpret well does not require a blocking out of preconceptions, because it is only through these preconceptions that "the meaning of the text can really be made to speak for us."[61] Thus it would be excluding the very thing that makes understanding possible. The past is not a passive object but a rich source of possibilities that emerge as we encounter it in terms of our horizon. To understand a text is always a matter of projecting a meaning, and this involves projecting "a meaning for the text as a whole as soon as some initial meaning emerges in the text."[62] Thus interpretation is a *process* of moving back and forth between part and whole as they mutually illuminate one another. This constitutes the famous hermeneutical circle. For Gadamer, in contrast to earlier writers, this "is not a 'methodological' dilemma, or circle," that is, a problem of whether we understand the part in terms of the whole text or the whole by first understanding the parts, but rather a basic and universal "structural element in understanding."[63]

The hermeneutical circle, in Gadamer's view, involves not only the relationship between part and whole but the relationship between the interpreter and the text. We approach a text with a "foreunderstanding," but this continually changes as the meaning of the text unfolds in this dialogue betwen text and interpreter. The meaning of a text, then, is directly linked to its significance for the interpreter. Likewise, he insists, as opposed to an argument such as that of Hirsch, that "understanding is always an interpretation, and hence interpretation is the explicit form of understanding."[64] Yet he goes further and maintains that not only are understanding and interpretation merely analytically distinct aspects of one thing but that understanding also "always involves something like the application of the text to be understood to the present situation of the interpreter" and thus he sees understanding, interpretation, and application as part of a single process.[65] Since "history is only present to us in light of our futurity,"[66] there is no separating the explanatory and practical aspects of historical interpretation. The horizon of the interpreter is simultaneously projected toward the past and future.

Gadamer's emphasis on understanding the past in terms of the present and future is balanced by a concern with maintaining an openness toward the past and tradition. He is disturbed by the approach of sociological theorists such as Jürgen Habermas whose concern with social change and the critique of ideology has led, he believes, to an exaggerated critical ideal that views all tradition and authority as wrong and that is informed by an image of "an anarchistic utopia."[67] Consciousness of effective history and reflection on bne's historicality serves to eliminate naive objectivism by being aware of prejudices and controlling preunderstanding. A critical stance, "that considers itself absolutely free of prejudice and independent, necessarily remains snared in illusions."[68] A critical attitude is important, but it is only one possible aspect of hermeneutical reflection. He insists that, if carried too far, it obscures the productive features of tradition as well as the traditional character of all understanding.

UNDERSTANDING: THEORY AND PRACTICE

Gadamer's hermeneutical theory pointedly challenges the assumption that understanding a text is primarily a matter of reconstructing an author's thoughts or intentions. It may help to make sense of Gadamer's position by viewing it both as one manifestation of a trend in contemporary philosophy away from the seventeenth and eighteenth century notion that the basic function of language is to express mental discourse or ideas and as a rejection of the more modern view that speech is a medium for conveying separate meaning. Although those who may be identified with this trend are by no means members of a single philosophical persuasion, they all, in one way or another, question the assumption that language is either a mode of representing ideas that constitute "the interface between the knower and the known"[69] or primarily an instrumental carrier of intersubjectively shared meanings regarding belief and knowledge which make communication possible. Instead, language is itself viewed as the interface between the knowing subject and the experience of reality and as an autonomous object of investigation. The result is potentially "a radical transformation in our modes of understanding."[70] There is an increasing recognition of arguments that knowledge inheres in "some linguistic entity, a text or discourse perhaps, regarded as an object in itself and not merely as the bearer of some antecedent meaning."[71]

In some respects, this trend is reflected in the position of those who identify themselves with the new history of political theory, since they emphasize the study of political languages and view political theory as a linguistic event. However, they are still bound at least to the residue of the assumption that the study of political language in the past is a way of gaining access to the prior thoughts, meanings, or intentions of actors. They recognize that there is a close tie between language and thought and that meanings are formulated and expressed in a public language. In this sense, following such philosophers as Wittgenstein and J. L. Austin, they would maintain that there are no private meanings, but they retain at least the form of an argument based on the assumption that language represents or expresses mental states and that the study of language is to recover these states. They still study the language of the past in order to recount the history of *ideas*. They do not approach the more radical position of individuals such as Michel Foucault who insist that any distinction between language and thought is untenable and that human phenomena are linguistic in character.[72] In many respects, Gadamer, following Heidegger, comes to a similar conclusion. What is to be understood is not an author, an idea, or even a meaning, since "Being that can be understood is language" and "it is of such a nature that of itself it offers itself to be understood." In this view, the speaker is really the instrument of language rather than language being a vehicle for a speaker's thought. He argues that "to be expressed in language does not mean that a second being is acquired. The way in which a thing presents itself is, rather, part of its own being."[73] The meaning of a text is not what is behind it but the claim that it presents to the reader.

Although it is quite reasonable to suggest that the positions of Gadamer and, for example, Hirsch represent alternative paradigms of interpretation, it is necessary to avoid setting up an artificial debate between those who hold that to understand a text is to decipher the meaning of the author, or retranslate the intention that the author translated into speech, and those who maintain that interpretation is a matter of understanding a text itself and not the person who wrote it. It could be argued that to some extent what is involved here is a difference in emphasis. Gadamer is not denying that the historical circumstances of a text are relevant for understanding it. He is not suggesting that interpretation depends on a whim of the interpreter or even that a concern with technique and method is not important for disciplines in the human sciences. What he does stress, however, is that interpretation would be sterile if texts were mere objects of investigation. Understanding is not simply a matter of achieving "technical virtuosity" in reading but "a genuine experience, i.e., an encounter with something that asserts itself as truth."[74] On the other hand those who concern themselves with method are not advocating that the substantive claims of a text or its significance for the reader be ignored but rather that the claim of truth of a text, or what it says, and its contemporary relevance cannot be reasonably discussed until its historical meaning is clarified.

Some attempts have been made to develop a hermeneutical theory which incorporates both points of view. Paul Ricoeur, for example, agrees in effect with those who view speech or oral discourse as basically the externalization of an intention and maintains that understanding is principally a matter of apprehending the dimensions of intended meaning. Ricoeur argues, however, that when discourse is written it undergoes a fundamental transformation. What was said becomes fixed and is no longer an event in a dialogic situation. In consequence, there is a "dissociation of the verbal meaning of the text and the mental intention."[75] This link is not abolished, but it becomes "distended and complicated," and the "text's career escapes the finite horizon lived by its author." At this stage, "what the text says now matters more than what the author meant to say, and every exegesis unfolds its procedures within the circumference of a meaning that has broken its moorings to the psychology of its author."[76] At the same time, the original reference or "aboutness" of discourse recedes, and the text creates a world of its own that emerges as it is confronted by the perspective of the interpreter and, at the same time, influences that perspective.[77] Finally, the text creates its own audience and is marked by the "universality of its address" as it is detached from the original addressee and opens itself up to interpretation by anyone who can read. Ultimately, as with Gadamer, this means that "to understand a text is not to rejoin the author."[78] For Ricoeur, the pragmatic differences between understanding oral and written discourse add up to viewing a text as a qualitatively distinct phenomenon.

The difficulty with Ricoeur's somewhat ecumenical approach, however, is that it tends to gloss over some root theoretical differences that may not be reconcilable. Although what separates an argument such as that of Gadamer from that of someone who views understanding as a matter of eliciting an author's meaning may be in part a matter of the focus of their concern or the extent to which they differentiate between written and oral speech, these positions are informed by salient differences regarding the theory of language. When Gadamer claims that the truth of texts "lies in what is said in them; and not in a meaning locked in the impotence of subjective particularity" and that what is said in a text "is not something that pertains to the speaker, but to what is spoken,"[79] he is enunciating a hermeneutial theory which may not be compatible with that of those who would equate understanding with the reconstruction of subjective meaning. Furthermore, the problem of interpretation involves much more than the differences between theories of interpretation.

A question must be posed about the relationship between the theories and the practice of interpretation. Earlier in this chapter, I suggested that what individuals such as Skinner and Pocock proposed as a method for the history of ideas was not a method at all in the sense of a procedure for practice but rather basically a philosophical account of the nature of interpretation. Although there is a sense in which any interpretative claim is based, either consciously or unconsciously, on certain assumptions about the nature of interpretation, there is still a fundamental logical difference between an argument *about* the character of textual interpretation—that is, an account of what does or what should take place in the course of interpreting a text—and *knowing how* to understand a text and evaluate interpretative claims. For example, Skinner's assumption that his theory of linguistic meaning yields a method for understanding texts in political theory is no more tenable than the idea that proficiency in everyday speech is predicated upon the philosophy of language or artistic skill upon knowledge of aesthetics. This is not to suggest that there is no relationship between hermeneutics and the practice of interpretation. Such practice is the object of hermeneutical investigation, and a descriptive or normative account of interpretation or historicity may in some way enhance interpretative practice or serve as a critical instrument for evaluating it. The possible relationships are many and varied. However, such an account is hardly the condition of such practice, or even the theoretical component of it, any more than theory and practice in science are based on the philosophy of science. Philosophical arguments about interpretation no more have a necessary relationship to the validity of a particular interpretation than arguments in the philosophy of science have for the standards of truth in scientific practice or the philosophy of religion has for the acceptance of theological doctrines. However, there is a special problem about the relationship between philosophy and the human sciences that often leads to confusion on this point.

The relationship between academic philosophy on the one hand and, for example, natural science, religion, and language on the other hand may be philosophically problematical, that is, it may be a matter of philosophical concern, but it very seldom raises a practical problem. This is in large measure because these activities were established as identifiable and autonomous practices prior to the establishment of the subfields in philosophy that study them. Despite the fact that philosophy may at certain times have some impact on these activities, the practice of these activities has tended to precede the philosophical analysis of it. The logic and epistemology of these activities are the objects of philosophical investigation. The situation has been, and continues to be, somewhat different as far as the relationship between formal philosophy and some of the human sciences and social sciences. Although certain of these "sciences" are distinct, or relatively distinct, fields of study, they are often not activities which are organized around any easily identifiable core of theory and practice. To a large extent, their history shows their continuing attempt to establish themselves as disciplined activities in the image either of natural science or of some alternative but comparable vision. Philosophical accounts of these activities have usually involved more an attempt to demonstrate what they or their method should be rather than an explication of what they are, and there has been an attempt in these fields to seek from philosophy an identity and a justification of their endeavors. They have turned to philosophy precisely because they sought to establish themselves as practices, and this is why the idea of method, when found in philosophy, has been so appealing. In the case of the history of ideas in general, as well as the history of political theory, the situation is quite clear. These labels do not refer to distinct modes of disciplined inquiry but rather designate a relatively disparate group of enterprises which, despite similarities, are often pursued in quite different ways with very different purposes. There can be little doubt that recent as well as past concern with historicity and method in the history of ideas is more an attempt to establish a practice than to purify one. This concern has brought the history of ideas into contact with the philosophy of interpretation and has made it difficult to sort out the boundaries between the practice of history and philosophical claims about it.

Much of hermeneutical theory—including the work of Dilthey, Collingwood, and more recent proponents of some species of the view that interpretation involves recovering the meaning of an author—is concerned with providing a philosophical rationale for the human sciences that would justify them as comparable to natural science, in the sense of achieving objective knowledge, and yet establish them as methodologically autonomous. Yet, despite the emphasis on differentiating between the human and natural sciences, the analysis has been burdened with a philosophical framework from the very philosophy it wished to combat, that is, the positivist representation of science as the application of method in attaining knowledge of objective facts. Both those who advocated that the human sciences emulate the natural sciences and those who attempted to demonstrate that the human sciences were methodologically distinct accepted the positivist view of natural science and the identification of science with methodism. What they wished to establish now was the autonomy of the historical method. Yet what is necessary to keep in mind is that this so-called method is a philosophical reconstruction of interpretation and not a technique for practice any more than the philosopher's account of scientific method provides the basis for scientific investigation.

Gadamer, more than some other philosophers dealing with these problems, recognizes this distinction between philosophical and practical methods or the difference between scientific practice and a philosophical claim about it. Yet he does not entirely escape this difficulty. Although he emphasizes his concern with the universal features of understanding that transcend all particular activities and specifically denies that he wishes to debate the methodological symmetry of the natural and human sciences, he continually insists that "the use of scientific methods does not suffice to guarantee truth"[80] in interpretation. Yet what he refers to as scientific methods is simply the positivistic view of natural science as the application of method to the explanation of objectively given observable facts. His rejection of method is in part a result of his belief that while "the object of the natural sciences can be described idealiter as what would be known in the perfect knowledge of nature . . . it is senseless to speak of a perfect knowledge of history, and for this reason it is not possible to speak of an object in itself towards which its research is directed."[81] It is doubtful that this is an accurate characterization of natural science; at least it sharply conflicts with much of the recent work in the philosophy of science associated with individuals such as Thomas Kuhn who suggest that there is no ultimate interpretation of nature or specification of the facts of science and the scientific method outside particular theoretical contexts. However, Gadamer's disclaimer about providing a method for historical inquiry must be taken seriously. He is attempting to say what interpretation is or, if it is to be authentic and escape the imposition of alien frameworks, must be rather than to prescribe a procedure. He is presenting a philosophical account of what constitutes or should constitute such studies.

Nevertheless, it is probably inevitable that both opponents and advocates of Gadamer's work will take his argument as a prescription for practice which embraces some sort of interpretative relativism and denies the possibility of making a valid claim about understanding a text. He will be read as recommending methodological anarchy, proclaiming every man his own interpreter, and giving up what Charles Beard termed the "noble dream" of historical objectivity. This would be a misconstrual of both what he is saying and the actual relationship between the philosophy and practice of interpretation. What, for example, earlier hermeneutical theory posed as a basic problem of interpretation, that is, neutralizing the effect of one's own horizon, Gadamer maintains is a fundamental condition of understanding. These are alternative philosophical claims about what goes on in understanding, and Gadamer is by no means offering a license to make interpretation a matter of taste by insisting that it always emerges from an encounter with the practical concerns of the interpreter. His rejection of method and the criterion of the *mens auctoris* as a basis for achieving a canonical interpretation of a text is similar to the rejection in the recent literature on the philosophy of science of the positivist representation of science as the progressive accumulation of knowledge about the natural world through the application of the hypothetico-deductive method and the testing of theories against theoretically independent facts. What is rejected is not the practice of science or its ideal of objectivity but rather a philosophical claim about science and scientific objectivity. Gadamer's philosophy of understanding no more undermines validity in interpretation than the arguments of individuals such as Kuhn subvert the basis of claims of truth in science. His argument is not a challenge to historicity but only to a particular philosophical claim about historicity.

To explain something requires being able to specify what kind of a thing is being explained, and this amounts to advancing a theory about the phenomenon which, in turn, provides the substantive criteria for what constitutes adequate explanation. Therefore, to make an interpretative claim about a text involves assumptions about what kind of a thing a text is. To some extent, hermeneutical philosophies may address this issue, but again there is a significant difference between a philosophy of interpretation and a theory which would specify the character of a text as a kind of phenomenon. Similarly, there is a difference between a philosophy of scientific explanation and a scientific theory, even though such a philosophy of explanation may say something about the nature of natural phenomena. Any approach to the practice of interpretation as well as any particular interpretative claims are ultimately based on certain notions about language and speech, and when hermeneutics addresses this issue it is dealing with questions of theoretical importance and relevance for interpretative practice, but seldom are these discussions of language and its exemplification in a text carried beyond summary characterizations and maxims. The focus is on explaining interpretation and only secondarily on the phenomena toward which interpretations are directed. In no field of disciplined inquiry is theory merely a matter of decision which precedes practice, let alone a decision based on the authority of a philosophical claim about practice. Theory and practice in inquiry are only analytically distinct, and theory emerges in the context of making and evaluating claims about the world, including claims about what a text says. Philosophy may factor out inquiry into theory, practice, method, and other categories and reassemble them in various ways in order to present a reconstruction of some mode of investigation, but this is not a recipe for the conduct of inquiry. Those who claim that they are offering a theory or method for the practice of the human sciences are almost always presenting a version of some philosophical account of inquiry in those fields. As important and interesting as such accounts and the differences between them may be, decisions about these matters are no more a prerequisite for the practice of interpretation than a decision about the character of meaning in language is a precondition of meaningful speech. People have been understanding one another, more or less, as long as human being has existed. Philosophies of interpretation are basically accounts of what happens when people do understand and what goes wrong when they do not. Such a philosophy, if correct, may in some way heighten the ability to understand, but not necessarily, any more than knowing about car engines makes one a good mechanic. It certainly does not provide a method.

There may be good reason to argue that much of the past scholarship in the study of the history of political theory was not in fact historical, whatever paradigm of historicity one might accept.

Although it might be tempting to suggest that a position such as Gadamer's may justify the practical concerns of much of that scholarship, since it places such great emphasis on tradition and the creative rendering of the past from the standpoint of the present, this is a dubious proposition. His argument does not support the idea of the existence of any particular tradition but only the notion that an interpreter always stands within a tradition of effective history. Further, although interpretation of the past is, in his view, always a practical endeavor conducted from within the horizon of the present, this is a thesis about the universal conditions of understanding and not an invitation to use past texts and the idea of the tradition in the rhetorical or strategic sense that Strauss, for example, employs them. The myth of the tradition would seem to violate the very openness toward the past that Gadamer advocates. It does, then, seem plausible for critics to claim that past approaches to the classic texts have not been historical and that a new, or at least revisionist, field of scholarship is potentially available. The classic works would become new phenomena. However, even apart from the problem of whether there is a discipline with an identifiable theory or theories which would support such interpretative inquiry and provide the core of interpretative practice, there is the question of what makes the study of this particular material worthy of such organized effort in either scholarship or teaching.

Despite its rejection of what it believes to be the unhistorical character of much of the past literature in the field, the legacy of the myth of the tradition is still quite apparent even among those who would view themselves as practitioners of a new history of political theory. They have inherited the classic texts as an object of study. Now, however, the rationale is gone, and a philosophy of interpretation cannot supply a substantive disciplinary matrix and research programs. In their various forms, the idea of the tradition and the myth of the tradition did provide a basis for the study of the history of political theory. They answered questions regarding why this material should be studied, what works should be the focus of research and teaching, how these works stood in relation to one another, how they should be approached, what political theory as an activity consisted of, and how political theory was related to political life. If there is to be a study of the history of political theory as part of the discipline of political science and as a coherent program of scholarship and teaching, these regional issues must be addressed. The idea of the tradition as it has been understood in the past can no longer be taken seriously as a paradigm for this field of study, but without a conception of the history of political theory as a particular subject matter and a clear idea of why it should be studied, the charge of unreflective antiquarianism that Easton and others incorrectly leveled against earlier scholars may now be valid.

NOTES

1. Quentin Skinner, "Meaning and Understanding in the History of Ideas," *History and Theory* 8 (1969): 48.

2. Ibid., pp. 28, 49.

3. John Dunn, "The Identity of the History of Ideas," *Philosophy* 43 (1968): 85, 86.

4. Ibid., p. 86.

5. Ibid., pp. 87, 88.

6. Ibid., p. 93.

7. Ibid., p. 92.

8. Ibid., p. 98.

9. Ibid., p. 99.

10. J. G. A. Pocock, *Politics, Language and Time* (New York: Atheneum, 1971), p. 9.

11. Ibid., p. 11.

12. Quentin Skinner, "Some Problems in the Analysis of Political Thought and Action," *Political Theory* 2 (August 1974): 280–81.

13. For a representative selection and discussion of such arguments, see Fred R. Dallmayr and Thomas A. McCarthy, eds., *Understanding and Social Inquiry* (Notre Dame: University of Notre Dame Press, 1977).

14. Skinner, "Meaning and Understanding in the History of Ideas," p. 48. See also Quentin Skinner, "Conventions and the Understanding of Speech Acts," *Philosophical Quarterly* 20 (1970): 118–38; "On Performing and Explaining Linguistic Actions," *Philosophical Quarterly* 21

(1971): 1–21; and " 'Social Meaning' and the Explanation of Social Action," in Peter Laslett and W. G. Runciman, eds., *Philosophy, Politics and Society*, Third Series (New York: Barnes and Noble, 1967).

15. Skinner, "Meaning and Understanding in the History of Ideas," p. 49.

16. Pocock, *Politics, Language and Time*, p. 15. See also, J. G. A. Pocock, "The History of Political Thought: A Methodological Inquiry," in Peter Laslett and W. G. Runciman, eds., *Philosophy, Politics and Society*, Second Series (New York: Barnes and Noble, 1962), pp. 183–202.

17. Ibid., pp. 15–16.

18. Ibid., p. 25.

19. Ibid., pp. 30–31.

20. See fn 60, Chapter I.

21. Both Skinner and Pocock make reference to Hirsch's argument. Eric D. Hirsch, *Validity in Interpretation* (New Haven: Yale University Press, 1967).

22. Ibid., pp. 3, 8.

23. Ibid., pp. 27, 45–46.

24. Ibid., p. 81.

25. E. D. Hirsch, Jr., *The Aims of Interpretation* (Chicago: University of Chicago Press, 1976), pp. 80, 146.

26. Ibid., p. 17.

27. See Friedrich Schleiermacher, *Hermeneutik*, 1833–1911, ed. Heinz Kimmerle (Heidelberg: Carl Winter, 1974). For a discussion of the hermeneutical tradition, see Richard E. Palmer, *Hermeneutics: Interpretation Theory in Schleiermacher, Dilthey, Heidegger, and Gadamer* (Evanston, Il.: Northwestern University Press, 1969).

28. See Wilhelm Dilthey, *Descriptive Psychology and Historical Understanding* (Hague: Nijhoff, 1977); *Pattern and Meaning in History* (New York: Harper, 1961). Also Rudolf A. Makkreel, *Dilthey: Philosopher of the Human Studies* (Princeton: Princeton University Press, 1975).

29. R. G. Collingwood, *The Idea of History* (New York: Oxford University Press, 1956), pp. 1, 3.

30. Ibid., pp. 9, 10.

31. R. G. Collingwood, *An Autobiography* (New York: Oxford University Press, 1970), p. 58; *The Idea of History*, p. 213.

32. Collingwood, *The Idea of History*, p. 215.

33. Collingwood, *An Autobiography*, p. 111.

34. Collingwood, *The Idea of History*, p. 215.

35. Ibid., p. 218.

36. Ibid., pp. 219, 304; Collingwood, *An Autobiography*, p. 111.

37. Collingwood, *The Idea of History*, p. 219.

38. Ibid., pp. 246–47.

39. Ibid., p. 320.

40. Ibid., p. 232.

41. Ibid., p. 248.

42. Hans-Georg Gadamer, *Truth and Method* (New York: Seabury, 1975), p. 90.

43. Ibid., pp. xiii, xvii.

44. Ibid., p. xix.

45. Ibid., pp. 408, 411.

46. Ibid., pp. 401, 364–65.

47. Hans-Georg Gadamer, *Philosophical Hermeneutics* (Berkeley: University of California Press, 1976), pp. 15, 16.

48. Gadamer, *Truth and Method*, p. 263; *Philosophical Hermeneutics*, pp. 9, 15.

49. Gadamer, *Truth and Method*, p. 230.

50. Ibid., pp. xxiii, 232.

51. Ibid., p. 267.

52. Ibid., p. 324.

53. Ibid., p. 273.

54. Ibid., pp. 264–65.

55. Ibid., pp. 107, 267–69, 289.

56. Ibid., p. 149.

57. Ibid., p. 110.

58. Ibid., p. 262.

59. Ibid., pp. 263, 264.

60. Ibid., p. 357.

61. Ibid., p. 358.

62. Ibid., p. 236.

63. Ibid., p. 261.

64. Ibid., p. 274.

65. Ibid., p. 275.

66. Gadamer, *Philosophical Hermeneutics*, p. 9.

67. Ibid., p. 42. See Jürgen Habermas, *Knowledge and Human Interests* (Boston: Beacon, 1971), and *Theory and Practice* (Boston: Beacon, 1973).

68. Gadamer, *Philosophical Hermeneutics*, pp. 93–94.

69. Ian Hacking, *Does Language Matter to Philosophy?* (New York: Cambridge University Press, 1975), p. 185.

70. Ibid., p. 159.

71. Ibid., pp. 181–82.

72. See, for example, Michel Foucault, *The Order of Things* (New York: Pantheon, 1971); *The Archaeology of Knowledge* (New York: Pantheon, 1972).

73. Gadamer, *Truth and Method,* p. 432.

74. Ibid., p. 445.

75. Paul Ricoeur, "The Model of the Text," *Social Research* 38 (1971): 534; see also "Ethics and Culture: Habermas and Gadamer in Dialogue," *Philosophy Today* 17 (1973).

76. Ricoeur, "The Model of the Text," p. 534.

77. Ibid., pp. 535, 536.

78. Ibid., p. 537, 547.

79. Gadamer, *Truth and Method,* p. 445.

80. Ibid., p. 446.

81. Ibid., p. 253.

Plato 428?–348? B.C.

V

Political Theory: Text and Action

> . . . the history of political theory is not the history of different answers given to one and the same question, but the history of a problem more or less constantly changing, whose solution was changing with it.
>
> *R. G. Collingwood*

THE STUDY OF THE CLASSICS:
WHAT AND WHY

The exposition, interpretation, evaluation, and teaching of the classic texts have themselves come to constitute a tradition, but a challenge to the myth of the tradition presents grave problems to the perpetuation of this academic activity in its customary form. As long as *the* tradition is accepted as significant, problems regarding its content and its implications for understanding the present can be taken as crucial, but if the idea of the tradition cannot be sustained, these issues lose their force. Once again questions are inevitably raised about whether the study of the history of political theory is anything more than a sterile historicism that detracts from a relevant and creative application of political thought to the problems of the present, and whether the amount of scholarship devoted to the meaning of the "great books" has not been extended beyond any reasonably justified limits.

Those who recommend what they conceive as a truly historical approach to these works might suggest that the myth of the tradition has obscured the actual meaning of the classic works and the genuine historical contexts and traditions to which they belong, and that consequently a whole field of revisionist scholarship is open to the researcher. In some respects this may be quite true, but also it may be doubtful that, apart from one or two exceptional cases, much more can be contributed to solving the historical puzzles surrounding the intentions and circumstances of these authors. It is at least questionable that such research is adequate to support a discipline or subdiscipline. The likelihood, for example, of deciding definitively whether Machiavelli's *Prince* was a piece of advice for aspiring political entrepreneurs, a prototype of modern political science, a tactic for gaining a job, a plea for a leader to unify Italy, a satire to expose the politics of the age, or all of these at once, is very small, and it is not at all clear what would be gained by an academic consensus on such issues. Despite their dissatisfaction with past scholarship, the new historians of political theory are heir to the research organized around the myth of the tradition. They reject the assumptions that originally justified this endeavor and are left to preside over the interpretation of a body of material which seems neither to possess a constitutive principle nor to evoke an immediate and apparent demand for concern. Despite their critique of their predecessors, recent historians persist in a search for what was crucial to earlier scholars, that is, the achievement of a canonical interpretation. However now the project is defended on the grounds of historical knowledge rather than its practical implications for politics.

For those who wish to maintain the history of political theory as a distinct field of study organized around the classical texts, a single compelling rationale is not easily established once the idea of the tradition no longer provides the context of interpretation and the criteria of selection. The process through which the basic works of the tradition were determined is probably impossible to reconstruct. It was largely a matter of the evolution of academic custom, and little more can be said with certainty than that these works were selected because they were taken to be part of the tradition and that the tradition was, in turn, the product of this selection. Once, however, there is an end to a consideration of these issues within the constraints of the myth of the tradition and the debates that have surrounded it since the 1950s, it should be apparent that the possible grounds for teaching and commenting on historical texts in political theory are rich and abundant. The problem of justifying this endeavor arose in the context of controversies in political science, and once the endeavor is removed from this context, there is little reason to suggest that it requires any more special vindication than other branches of human studies.

Much of past scholarship on the history of political theory must be seriously qualified but is by no means totally nullified by rejecting the assumptions of the myth of the tradition. Not only has some of this literature contributed to an understanding of particular texts on their own terms, but there is nothing at all untoward about utilizing the classic works for exploring certain philosophical issues of politics and seeking insights into modern political practice. What is important is that the meaning of the past is not made to bear the burden of justifying critical judgments about politics and that the pretension of presenting the significance of all previous thought is avoided. The works of individuals such as Plato, Machiavelli, Hobbes, and Rousseau may not constitute some natural whole, but there are numerous reasons why they might be considered together as an object of study.

Without subscribing to any form of the myth of the tradition or accepting the notion of the great dialogue literally, it is perfectly possible to approach much of this literature as a series of perspectives on perennial and fundamental issues of political life which challenge and teach the reader to think about these issues. Nor is any injustice necessarily done if these works are treated topically as instances of various types of argument concerning basic political concepts such as obligation, authority, justice, power, and liberty. Finally, it is not necessarily naive to look at this literature as a source of political wisdom or even of basic truths about political things, and even the notion of deriving empirical hypotheses about politics from these works is not inherently absurd. What is unfortunate is that many of the more modest recommendations for studying the classics have been proposed by political scientists who wished to depreciate their importance. Consequently, such recommendations have been held in contempt by those who saw the divination of the tradition as an apocalyptic issue and as the secret to the fate of Western civilization. There are also numerous historical justifications for studying this literature which range from discovering the impact of certain works on political institutions and ideas to locating these works and their mode of discourse in a particular historical setting. There is no requirement that these works be relevant to a current political problem, and since many are literary masterpieces, their internal structure and meaning present intriguing problems of textual analysis and criticism just as the purpose and origin of a particular work may provide an interesting historical puzzle. They are, after all, artifacts that merit the concern of archaeologists of knowledge. The problem is not so much one of finding legitimate reasons, both practical and academic, for investigating this literature and rationalizing the choice of works for study as it is a problem of mistaking the selection for a self-defined chronological tradition that has shaped modern politics, believing that the excavation of this tradition holds a solution to a contemporary crisis, or any of the other aspects of the syndrome associated with the myth of the tradition. The question of why the classics might be studied, however, is closely tied to the problem of precisely what it is that is being studied.

There is a justification for speaking of this literature, which has come down to us by academic convention, as a distinct genre and even as a tradition if we are careful to acknowledge that these are analytical reconstructions created from the standpoint of certain present concerns and criteria. Similarly, there is good reason to designate political theory as an activity and to discuss the political theorist as a kind of actor as long as it is recognized that these are ideal typifications and not preexistent historical objects. From this perspective, the question of which works belong to political theory and, particularly, which deserve to be considered classics, does not admit of any very definitive answer. Although my purpose in the following pages is to develop a model which would in some respects provide an alternative to the idea of the tradition as a basis for approaching many of the texts that have customarily constituted the subject matter of the history of political theory, it would be presumptuous to claim that this model is anything more than one possible pedagogical recommendation.

My basic thesis is not very contentious. It is simply that certain of the classic works are exemplary instances of a creative mind's encounter and engagement with the problem of political order and that, in terms of their content and the circumstances of their production, they bear certain family resemblances, and possess certain common motifs, which make it reasonable to construct a paradigm of political theory and the political theorist to which specific works conform in varying degrees. To designate this literature as a particular type which can be distinguished in some important respects as *sui generis* is neither to specify some common literary form which the authors adopted nor to identify some activity in which they intentionally and reflectively participated, but rather to recognize that although these works may be assigned to various conventional categories based on their intrinsic genre and the historical context to which they belonged, there are good reasons for approaching them in terms of the extrinsic genre "political theory." Although it may be perfectly adequate to designate, for example, Aeschylus's *Oresteia* as Greek tragedy or Shakespeare's *Hamlet* as Elizabethan drama, it is not adequate to designate Plato's *Republic* simply as philosophy or Machiavelli's *Prince* as a species of the mirror-of-princes literature. To some extent, the approach that I am recommending involves both analytical and historical claims. The attributes which I ascribe to political theory and the political theorist are idealizations, but they are historically derived. This is not an a priori ideal type but one whose essential elements are drawn from an analysis of certain classic works. Some texts can be distinguished by the extent to which they do *not* conform to this model (those of Burke, John Stuart Mill, etc.), and I do not suggest that every writer who might conceivably be considered within the category of Western political thought can be usefully approached from this perspective. No attempt is made to exhaust the themes introduced in the next section, and what is offered is more an invitation to a particular mode of thinking about this material than any set of elaborated interpretative claims.

THEORY AND THEORIZING

I would argue that Plato may be fruitfully considered as the prototypal political theorist. In this respect, I am to a certain extent agreeing with the convention of designating him as the first major political theorist, but my point is not that Plato was the initiator of the tradition. Perhaps many later theorists were in some manner influenced by Plato or, even if they disagreed with him, aware of a certain affinity between his concerns and theirs, but what I wish to suggest is that the characteristics of political theory as an ideal type that I will attempt to delineate are most fully represented in Plato's work and that it is possible to draw interesting parallels between his work and that of such figures as Machiavelli, Hobbes, and Rousseau. With regard to Rousseau, there may be reason to suggest that the similarity of his work to that of previous theorists does have a strong traditional element in the limited sense that it may to some extent be a more conscious replication of what he perceived as the principal features of the great treatises on politics in Western culture. Some of the similarities of form and meaning that I wish to point out in these works were adopted by Rousseau.

There are few more frequent distortions in the textbooks and other secondary literature on political theory than the implication that Plato steps on to the scene without precedent. Often little attention is given to the intellectual context of his work and its relation to that of Homer, Hesiod, Aeschylus, Thucydides, and even Socrates. Yet, apart from the form in which they wrote or presented their ideas, there is at least one very significant difference which does distinguish Plato and characterizes much of the literature that has come to be accepted as classics of political theory. While Thucydides, for example, may have attempted to convey, in his reconstruction of the course of the Peloponnesian War, the causes of political disorder and the conditions of a healthy society, and while the historical Socrates may have exposed the illusions and hypocrisy of Athens, Plato not only diagnosed the ills of the city and chided its intellectuals and politicians but confronted the polis with a radical vision of a new society and concerned himself in some detail with various dimensions, both theoretical and practical, of the problem of realization.[1] However, to fully understand this difference, it is necessary to read the *Republic,* and others of Plato's writings often taken to be philosophical, in a manner quite different from the normal approach of a contemporary philosophical analysis of politics. In nominating Plato as an archetype, there is the danger of suggesting that political theorists are best understood as philosophers, and although this designation may have its point, considerable qualification is necessary.

Although political theory and political philosophy are often used interchangeably, political theorist as used here does not designate someone who merely treats politics philosophically, even if philosophical is used broadly to include critical, systematic, reflective, analytical, evaluative, perscriptive, and the like. It would be difficult to make a case for why Machiavelli or Rousseau, for example, should be labeled philosophers in any significant sense that would reflect contemporary criteria of application. Yet the identification with philosophy does suggest an important characteristic of political theory: its location outside the realm of political action. This does not mean that the attitude of the theorist is merely contemplative. The relationship of political theory to political action is complicated, and much of the problem of understanding works in political theory revolves around their relationship to political practice not only as a persistent theme and concern in this literature but as an aspect of the context of its production. In a very fundamental sense, the criterion for distinguishing political theory as a particular kind of creative activity and body of literature is the degree to which the vision of the theorist is inseparable from the problem of restructuring political society in terms of that vision. Like that of the artist, it is a vision that demands incarnation and requires public expression.

Although my use of the word theory is somewhat arbitrary, and largely a matter of academic convention, the etymology is instructive for elaborating this representation of the political theorist.[2] Theory derives from the classical Greek word *theorein* which means, literally, to watch or look at. It is probably closely related to *thaumazein* which means to wonder or admire and *theasthai,* another word for look, which carries this sense of wonder and signifies a religious experience and the awe that human beings experienced as they gazed on the spectacle of the beauty and perfection of the gods and the cosmos. Aristotle, and Greek philosophy generally, equated philosophy and theory with wonder, and Plato defines philosophers as individuals "for whom truth is the spectacle of which they are enamored." A "sense of wonder is the mark of the philosopher. Philosophy indeed has no other origin, and he was a good genealogist who made Iris the daughter of Thaumas."[3] Cicero reports a story in which Pythagoras, the mathematician and philosopher, explained his way of life by comparing it to that of those who came to the Olympic games not as participants but only as spectators.[4] For Aristotle, *theoria* means intellectual contemplation, an activity in accordance with *sophia* or the virtue of that aspect of the mind which is directed toward the eternal. Aristotle maintained that the activity of contemplation produced the greatest happiness and involved a divorce from practical affairs such as politics. For Aristotle, the philosopher is still bound to the polis in that the city provides the material base and the leisure necessary for the theoretical life (*bios theoretikos*) and in that he owes the city something for making such a life possible, but although theory might benefit politics, it involves a transcendence of the polis and is distinctly superior to the life of the citizen.[5]

Although the life of the philosopher and that of the political actor are distinguished in Plato's work and although in principle, as well as existentially, there is a tension between these ways of life, it is also apparent that for Plato not only is politics diminished by the absence of the philosopher but that philosophy demands fulfillment in practical life and in ruling or in the authorship of political institutions. The conflict between theory and politics in Plato's work and life should not obscure the attraction of theory to politics. In this respect, Plato's notion of theory may more closely reflect the original meaning of *theoria*. Originally theorist (*theoros*) designated an observer of a religious festival and was applied to someone dispatched by the polis to consult the oracle at Delphi or to visit a neighboring city and report about religious rituals or honor local divinities. The theorist observes a spectacle (*thea*) and what emerges is an understanding or account (*theorema*). Eventually *theoros* was used as a more general term for spectator, and particularly a spectator of athletic contests and dramatic presentations at the Games, and for someone commissioned to travel to foreign lands and bring back information. Finally, *theoria* was appropriated by philosophy and equated with the contemplation of the heavens in the "theatre" of the cosmos, but, even with Aristotle, it never entirely loses its original sense as an *intermediary* activity which is still so apparent in Plato. The theorist may be detached from the polis, but he mediates between truth and politics.

The theorist is often a person who in some respect stands outside, or has been forced outside, the sphere of normal political action and denied access to participation in politics and public life, or at least has been barred from a satisfactory mode of participation. Plato was destined by birth and inclination to assume a significant place in the political community, but while he "cherished like many another the hope of entering upon a political career," he found himself continually thwarted. He "gazed upon the whirlpool of public life" and the succession of progressively more corrupt regimes until he "felt dizzy." Even when Athens executed Socrates, "the justest man of his time," Plato continued to hold out hope for the propitious moment when he might have an opportunity to engage in creative action, but at last he was required to conclude that all existing governments were bad and almost beyond redemption.[6] The dramatic story of the death of Socrates in Plato's early dialogues not only represents a historical confrontation between philosophy and politics but probably also symbolizes a crisis in Plato's own life and his banishment from public involvement in Athens. It signifies the death of his own political life and his retreat to the Academy and to Sicily as a field of action. It was probably in these circumstances that Plato turned to philosophy, but not so much in flight from, or as an alternative to, politics as in search of a practical answer to the problem of social order and disorder. While there may be some point in isolating the *Republic, Statesman,* and *Laws* as Plato's political dialogues, there are good reasons to suggest that all of the dialogues are political, at least in that they are part of the confrontation between the truth of philosophy and the opinions of Athenian politics. He was not simply a philosopher who, like Aristotle, entered philosophy as a vocation and way of life (which Plato had helped to establish) and approached politics as one object of analysis, albeit a principal one, among other objects in the world, but rather someone who sought from philosophy a basis for the reconstruction of political life. Aristotle retained the idea of political science as a practical science in that its objective, unlike that of the theoretical sciences, was not merely to understand phenomena but to understand them for the purpose of changing or controlling them. Yet for Aristotle the realities of politics presented themselves as objects of science prior to any demand for their transformation while for Plato the demand for transformation was inseparable from the search for knowledge. It should be no surprise that the relationship between philosophy and politics, or knowledge and power, is a consistent theme in Plato's work as well as the focus of his practical ventures in advising the tyrant Dionysius of Syracuse and of the activities of many of his students in the Academy.

Yet although political theory is never severed from a concern with reordering society, there is a sense in which, as both activity and text, it becomes a substitute for political action, or even a kind of political action itself. Precluded from that measure of immortality that falls to the statesman and other public actors whose deeds and words are remembered by society, the theorist, like Thucydides who through his history of the rise and decline of Athenian power proclaims himself the recorder of the "greatest movement yet known in history," seeks immortality in producing a work of universal understanding of political things that will be a "possession for all time."[7] To some extent, theorists view their work as such a possession in that it is a literary monument to their intelligence, but they also hope that it will have a practical effect on political life if it should come into the right hands at the proper moment. Plato's construction of a hypothetical city in the *Laws* is both a reflection of what he might have undertaken if given the opportunity and a model for future legislators. Machiavelli, his political career with the Florentine republic cut short by the return to power of the Medici who imprisoned and tortured him, wrote the *Prince, Discourses,* and other works in forced retirement while always seeking a return to public life. He laments "the great and unmerited sufferings inflicted" on him "by a cruel fate," and, as he says of his situation in the comic play *Mandragola,* which portrays in dramatic form much of what he states about men and politics in the *Prince*, "the world's indifference alone restrains him from attempting to display his talents in a better way."[8] In his writings, the theorist often plays out a kind of private politics. He is the alienated individual who, like Rousseau, never succeeds in finding a city that meets the demands of his psyche or a place in which to engage in creative public action and thus constructs a society in words that fulfills the requirements which he understands as essential to sustain human well-being. It is often because he is denied a creative role in public life that he, like Rousseau, chooses "to write on politics." This writing often becomes a surrogate for action. "If I were a prince or a legislator I should not waste time in saying what wants doing; I should do it, or hold my peace."[9] Yet the relevance of what he says extends beyond the polis of his mind and his hopes for future recognition.

It has become almost axiomatic that many of the seminal works in political theory have been responses to existential political crises and, as Hobbes said of his own undertaking, "occasioned by the disorders of the present time."[10] It is in the midst of political or social disintegration that the role of the theorist emerges, and in this situation he sees not only danger but an opportunity for a creative reconstruction of political life. Yet his response is not simply a reflection of what we may now discern as political disorder such as the decline of Athens to which Plato addressed himself, the disunity of Italy at the end of the fifteenth century which absorbed Machiavelli, the English civil wars which formed the context of Hobbes's work, the morbidity of society and regime in France which Rousseau countered with the *Social Contract,* or the conditions of nineteenth century capitalism which prompted Marx's revelation of a new society both immanent and imminent in the historical process. These are merely the symptoms of what he sees as a deeper malady in society. His response is often a response to personal denial, yet it is not simply a matter of personal deprivation. His crisis and society's crisis are closely bound up with one another, and this is true not only in the sense that his exclusion is a product of what is happening in society. His suffering comes out of the sickness of the collectivity, but it is this bond which gives rise to a regenerative force directed back toward society.

Despite his isolation, the theorist is in some respects closer to the community than the everyday political actor. Although excluded from participation, he, like the Hebrew prophet, comes to see himself as the personification of the community. He feels the wounds of society more deeply partly because of this very exclusion and perceives more objectively, through his detachment, the condition of society. Although his attitude may at times appear to be almost one of hate and a willingness to do great violence to society, such as when Plato suggested a need to wipe the slate clean before undertaking a new beginning, it is a hatred for what has befallen the polity. Machiavelli's statement that he loved his native city more than his own soul could well express the sentiment of most theorists. His position is one of suffering.[11] He, like Socrates or the prophet, is the suffering servant, the pilgrim in a corrupt society who bears within himself the painful truth of the source of political disorder. Yet, as in all tragedy, suffering brings wisdom, and he views himself ultimately as the repository of a new idea of order, as the remnant of truth in society, and as the carrier of the secret of redemption.

The crisis, however, is more than political and more than personal. What the theorist perceives, or alleges, is not merely the breakdown of political order but literally a cosmic rupture, and a basic concern of political theory is the healing of that breach. Well before the emergence of theoretical consciousness in Western culture, the city had represented the home of human being in the world and linked society simultaneously to heaven and nature and integrated the individual with society. It was the breakdown of the symbolic form of the integral myth that had characterized those civilizations of the ancient world such as Egypt and Mesopotamia, as well as the Minoan and Mycenaean cultures that had preceded classical Greece, which brought about the recognition of mortality for both the individual and society. With the rending of that unity of the universe and that compression of life into the present which had characterized the mythic vision, society fell into history. This was a realm of decay where things moved in a line from beginning to end in contrast to the sempiternal cyclical rhythm of nature. All aspects of life became a journey between past and future where

humanity became progressively conscious of itself and the autonomous but alienated character of its existence. Individuals became
aware of themselves as authors of their actions, and collectively
aware of themselves as *homo faber* and aware of their responsibility
for order and disorder in society. Political theory was one kind of
response to the problem of historical existence, and it was a response that never entirely cast off its mythic past. It retained the
idea of the space of the city as the answer to the place of human
beings in the world and as the medium which bound together
heaven and earth and society and nature. Certainly what most
clearly distinguishes the political theorist is that he sees political
order as the answer to the basic problem of the human condition.
The vision of the theorist reflects the experience of historical decline and cosmic crisis, and his vision is one of the restoration of
order but a restoration that is informed by a new truth.

It is often argued that classical writers such as Thucydides,
Plato, and Aristotle had a cyclical view of history, but this is a crucial misreading and not at all representative of Greek thought from
Homer to Polybius. They had a cyclical view of natural time based
on the movement of the cosmos, but the pathos of history was that
society had been expelled from the cosmos. Human being and
human artifacts were bound within the realm of meaningless and
ceaseless change which was in sharp contrast to the eternity of
that which surrounded them. Here only Promethean *techne* could
save, and only then within definite limits. Although the Hebrews
and early Christians were able to find meaning in history and see it
as the manifestation of a sacred plan and although the later Christians, embracing an Augustian philosophy, believed that God
would release them from the meaningless cycles of history through
grace, the Greeks provided the intellectual framework within
which most of political theory would move, and it was a framework
of thought marked by a continual tension between history and social order. The idea of creating political order and in some measure
transcending history was the dream of the theorist. It was a majes-
tic enterprise through which an individual might not only gain immortality for himself but save society. Here an individual might
approximate, within the dispensation alloted to a mortal, the eter-

nity of cosmic creation and become the rival and emulator of God and the completer of the universe. Sometimes the great political theorists are identified as system-builders, but this emphasis on system (whether in Aristotle, St. Thomas Aquinas, or Hobbes) is a reflection of an attempt to reintegrate political order and the cosmos. It is this confrontation with the ineluctable character of historical existence that most clearly illuminates an essential motive of political theory, the concern with restructuring political space in order to annul political time.[12]

The philosophical polis in Plato's *Republic* appears dramatically in the text between a symbolic reconstruction of the rise and decline of Athenian politics and a hypothetical account of the degeneration of political regimes, and the model city in the *Laws* is preceded by an archaeology of political order and disorder in Greece. Similarly, the discussion of the demands of political rule in the *Statesman* is juxtaposed to a mythohistorical tale which looks backward from the degradation of contemporary politics. The creation of political order is a divine activity that brings order and meaning out of the randomness of history and temporal succession. The tension between political order and history so evident in Plato is rendered more discursively by Aristotle in his notion of a science of politics that could be applied in a variety of ways to create, reform, or merely sustain political society in a sublunar universe of constant change where unique human events succeed one another against a background of universal cosmic recurrence.

When Aristotle said that "man is by nature an animal intended to live in a polis," and that "the polis exists by nature,"[13] he did not mean that political society was the product of biological processes or that human beings were inevitably inclined to live in a polis or participate in politics. His point was that only in a polis and its educational structure could an individual lead an ethical life and reach the full potential of human being. Political society is natural to men, but it does not come into existence naturally as a product of biological nature. Political science and the political art of the statesman are required precisely because the polis is not a biological organism but a human artifact which rises above the order of time corresponding to natural processes and, to the extent that it is successful, transcends historical time which is measured by political change. Although some associations, such as the family, emerge by instinct and for the purpose of subsistence, the polis is a distinctly human form of association, and, according to Aristotle, the ,first creator of such a community was the author of the greatest good. Yet although the nature of human being demands the polis, the polis does not appear automatically any more, and even less, than the acorn necessarily reaches its potential as an oak tree. While nature, cosmic nature, is the principle of movement and actualization in the biological world and moves things, in ideal circumstances, toward their natural end, human action and artifice are the principles of emergence and movement in politics. Although other theorists may not agree with Aristotle's basic assumptions in many respects, they do agree with his assessment of political order as the product of human art, and despite their arguments about forms of social life as the epiphenomena of deterministic historical processes, this idea is by no means absent from the work of thinkers such as Hegel and Marx.

For Machiavelli, the study of history might provide evidence of principles underlying human action and politics, but history and time were synonymous with decay and change. This was the realm of *fortuna* where only *virtu* could provide a remedy for the fragility of human affairs which are always "in a state of perpetual movement, always either ascending or declining."[14] Ultimately, he believed, only the skill that flowed from his principles for organizing the body politic, his "new route," would be successful within the limitations of any human art.[15] For Hobbes, time is the symbol of decay, and it is not merely a metaphor. History is a realm where reality or being itself loses coherence, and most theorists would agree with Hobbes that "the present only has a being in nature."[16] The problem is to create a political body and preserve it from internal corruption and the flux of history, but this requires a "very able architect." The constitution of political society is naturally ontologically deficient in that it is "mortal, and subject to decay, as all other earthly creatures are," but at the same time the aim of the theorist is well-characterized as an attempt "to make this constitution . . . everlasting."[17] Machiavelli recognized that "all the things of this world have a limit to their existence" but that they can at least "run the entire course ordained for them by Heaven" if they "do not allow their body to become disorganized" and this is the aim of his political science.[18] Rousseau affirmed that "everything upon the earth is in continual flux. Nothing retains a form that is constant and fixed."[19] The political order suffers the same fate. Rousseau as well as Plato recognized that human beings and what they create are grounded in the natural world of inevitable change. Decay is "the natural and inevitable tendency of the best constituted governments," and we should "not even dream of making it [government] eternal." There are limits to the degree to which matter can sustain form, yet the theorist does not view this confrontation with political matter as hopeless. Human behavior remains a part of nature and subject to nature's laws, yet it is also subject to artifice and this, Rousseau affirms, is the province of the theorist. The goal is to create a virtual political nature.

> The body politic, as well as the human body, begins to die as soon as it is born, and carries in itself the causes of its destruction. But both may have a constitution that is more or less robust and suited to preserve them a longer or shorter time. The constitution of man is the work of nature; that of the state the work of art. It is not in men's power to prolong their own lives; but it is for them to prolong as much as possible the life of the State, by giving it the best possible constitution. The best constituted state will have an end; but it will end later than any other, unless some unforeseen accident brings about its untimely destruction.[20]

Although theory as literature, the creation of a city in speech, may become in some respects a surrogate for political action and an actual political creation, it is not simply compensatory fantasy or merely neurotic displacement born of frustration in which the theorist plays out a dream as creator and manipulator, although it may be all of these. It is not just that the theorist, confronting what he believes to be a corrupt society, responds with an inverted image of reality in which the decadent structures are imaginatively replaced by a utopia, although it may be this too. The great works in political theory are intricate literary pieces with manifold levels of symbolism, but what is often neglected in commentaries on the history of political philosophy is the serious purpose of the theorist with regard to realizing his vision and the extent to which, although his claims are intended to be universal and timeless, he addresses himself to particular political problems and not to abstract academic issues. He is not simply normative or prescriptive, and follows Aristotle in the belief that a political science is not merely a theoretical or contemplative endeavor. Even Rousseau, in many ways the most academic of political theorists, engaged, for example, in drafting constitutions for Poland and Corsica. Marx's charge that "the philosophers have only *interpreted* the world" while "the point, however, is to *change* it" is sometimes taken as a crucial juncture in the history of political theory where philosophy has turned into ideology. In fact, it is a motive as essential to Plato as to Marx. Theory and practice may be in tension but they are never divorced.

A historian of ideas might claim to find common concerns in Thomas More's *Utopia* and Plato's *Republic*, and, at a certain level of abstraction, this might be credible. Both were critics who deplored the conditions of their time and reflected in their works a sense of rage against the values that had come to dominate both rulers and ruled, and each drew a picture of an alternative society and agonized over the problem of the relationship between knowledge and power and their place in the politics of the age. Yet there are significant differences. Plato's architectonic vision was the product of a passionate desire to reconstruct political space and regenerate political time in a way that More's didactic satire was not. The political theorist is not simply a political thinker, a person who intellectualizes about politics. Many political thinkers would recoil from action, particularly the extraordinary action contemplated by a theorist, and they would be frightened or embarrassed by the demiurgic vision of the theorist. It is much more than a difference between radical and conservative attitudes. The theorist, unlike Seneca in his confrontation with Nero or Thomas More in his relationship to Henry VIII, is not a person who admonishes and remonstrates against those in power and then commits suicide or dies in public defense of his principles. The theorist who, like Plato, views himself as having received the "divine sign" as the instrument of truth and a new political reality,[22] and who believes that the fate of that truth is closely bound up with his ability to manipulate men of power, is not so quick to choose martyrdom. The careers of men such as Plato, Machiavelli, Hobbes, and Locke are marked by secrecy, craft, and other forms of dissembling which are employed in order to carry out what they conceive as their appointed task.

The distinction is clearly evident in the difference between Socrates and Plato, or, in a literary sense, in the distance between the Socrates of Plato's earlier dialogues, his diminished role in the later dialogues, and finally his replacement by the Athenian stranger in the *Laws* where Plato concerns himself most directly with practical problems of structuring society. Socrates is a critic and his life exemplifies the conflict between philosophy and politics, but he is a part of society and eventually unwilling to escape his sentence of death in respect for the sanctity of the laws of the polis. Yet the theorist is caught up in a higher mission and tends, like Plato, to refuse the role of physician to a sick society and to seek an opportunity to participate in a new beginning. He does not resign himself to sacrifice. In a period when the social cosmos has "run down," the "true Statesman" may not rule, but he is the vehicle of truth and the only means for the Idea to enter history. In these circumstances, he cannot risk "his life in vain without any hope of accomplishing anything."[23]

It is the problem of actualization, the problem of how to transform social behavior and institutions in the image of a new vision of order, that haunts political theory. A failure to fully recognize this crucial concern characterizes most of the scholarly commentaries on the history of political thought. While Socrates, after elaborating the character of the philosopher's polis in the *Republic*, concludes that "nowhere on earth" is there such a city and that "it makes no difference whether it exists now or ever will come into being" since the philosopher may keep "his eyes fixed on the constitution in his soul,"[24] it is a mistake to assume that he is giving an answer to the meaning of the *Republic* or his intention in the dialogue. The issue at that point is the stance of a philosopher in a corrupt society. Plato, in fact, points out that the philosopher who simply keeps to his business in an alien atmosphere "would not have accomplished any very great thing," and Plato's personal statement is that "I feared to see myself at last nothing but words . . . a man who would never willingly lay hand to any concrete task."[25] Once we cease to look at the *Republic* as a utopian tract and to approach it as if it were merely modern philosophic analysis in poetic form, it is possible to see that Plato's principal concern is to explore the many issues revolving around the extent to which political matter can be ordered by knowledge. In the cosmology in the *Timaeus* he considers the limits to which God, in creating the universe, could confer eternity on the random motions of chaos, and he concludes in the *Republic* that the creation and maintenance of the philosophical state is as unlikely as the transformation of matter into Idea or time into eternity. Finally, in the *Laws,* Plato turns not so much to a consideration of a second-best state, since the *Republic* never really elaborated any concrete institutional order at all, as to the problem of how to construct a regime that would reflect the wisdom of the true statesman but, at the same time, take account of the demands of the matter that must sustain the form. The recalcitrant character of political matter, the extent to which it is malleable and subject to art, and its inevitable revenge that brings about the dissolution of the body politic are principal themes in the work of every theorist.

Probably no political theorist has received more attention in the literature on the history of political theory than Machiavelli. He has been represented in various ways, usually according to some version of the myth of the tradition, as the originator of the theory of power politics, a rebel against classical morality and a counselor of evil, an advocate of political deceit, the first empirical political scientist, a realist, a humanist, a satirist, etc. All these categories are largely judgmental impositions that often obscure what may have been Machiavelli's actual concern with raising up a hero who would be the instrument for the liberation of Italy from the forces that had reduced that country "to slavery and degradation."[26] The "prince" would be the founder of a new republican order grounded on principles of organization that would enable it to achieve a kind of permanence in motion that transcended previous political forms. With Machiavelli, as with other theorists, it is not simply the problem of actualization as a theoretical issue with which they are concerned but the strategy of actualization; not only the principles of political transformation but the tactics for implementation are woven into their works and are often a function of the work itself, as with Machiavelli's chapter on conspiracies in the *Discourses*. Some of Plato's dialogues, including the *Republic*, as well as Machiavelli's *Discourses* were probably circulated among, and read to, political dissidents and calculated to instigate political change.

The apparently abstract character of Hobbes's writing has been matched by the abstractness of the commentaries on his work. In their haste to elevate individuals such as Hobbes and Locke to the rank of systematic philosophers, critics have played down their involvement in partisan politics and their circumstantial concerns.[27] Historians of political theory have become lost in the philosophical bowels of the *Leviathan*. Interpreting this work has become a matter of tracing out what they conceive as Hobbes's chain of deductive reasoning, searching for the key to his theory of obligation, debating the degree of his authoritarianism, atheism, and scientism, picking away at the intricacies of his version of the social contract, and considering the extent of his revision of traditional natural law. These are reasonable and legitimate objects of analysis, but focusing on such issues often leads to a neglect of Hobbes's theoretical adventure and the actual content and purpose of the *Leviathan* in favor of the many issues that the work may evoke and to which it may, from one perspective or another, be construed as a response. Although Hobbes said, regarding his discourses on politics, that "whether they come into the sight of those that have power to make use of them or be neglected by them, or not, concerneth my particular interests, at this day, very little," he did not come easily to "the point of believing this my labor, as useless as the commonwealth of Plato" and he hoped that his work would "fall into the hands of a sovereign" who would make its principles a matter of "public teaching."[28] There is often a failure to recognize that throughout the work Hobbes addresses himself to a series of strategic questions concerning the creation and implementation of a new communal myth which could sustain a structure of political authority and that the content of that myth is the idea of the "social contract" in *Leviathan*. What the theorist seeks is a new political reality, and in the course of this search he undercuts, at first symbolically, the grounds of existing reality. He presents a challenge not only to particular institutions but to the vision of the world that supports them, and this is often what leads to his exclusion from society.

It is this exclusion of the theorist that is in part the source of his sense of objectivity and sometimes of his actual ability to see the fate of society to which those around him are blind. It was only Thucydides, for example, the exiled general disengaged from the events in which he had once participated, who saw the Peloponnesian War as a total phenomenon and as the context of the rise and fall of Athenian power. It was Hobbes who saw in the turmoil of seventeenth century England the possibility of a fall into a state of nature. It was Marx who discerned, in the struggles arising out of modern industrialism, the relationship between alienation and domination. Yet the burden of this role of articulating the nature of disorder and exposing the future is perceived as a terrifying responsibility, and, when joined with a new vision of politics, it is often a role that society will not tolerate. Like the Hebrew prophet who, in chastizing king and subjects, tried to bring Israel to a consciousness of its defection from its principles and the consequences of this defection, the theorist attempts to expose the roots of disorder, and sometimes it is a disorder which is not yet visible. Yet unlike the prophet, the theorist who points out the disease of psyche and city lacks Mosaic authority and has no established role in society, and his critique of existing institutions and his vision of a new order reach the community as a threat from a subversive. The fear of reprisal that haunted men such as Hobbes and Locke and prompted them to flee their countries and occasionally to write obliquely was not merely a paranoid delusion. Sometimes their difficulties were the result of their political involvements as much as, or more than, their theoretical activity, but, even from their own perspective, their practical and symbolic actions are not easily disentangled.

The theorist and his message have usually been rejected by society, and Plato's discussion of the philosopher whose life is threatened by the city presents a paradigm of this relationship and represents the curtailment of his intellectual and political life by Athens. The theorist sees his enterprise, in Rousseau's words, as one of "setting myself up against all that is nowadays most admired," and he expects "no less than a universal outcry against me."[29] Only in retrospect does the relevance of his insights emerge clearly. Maybe in time the ideas of the theorist in some way or another find their way into the realm of political action and transform the manner in which people think and act politically, but the link between theory and action is a tenuous one, just as every theorist has realized. One of the most striking characteristics of political theory has been its profound lack of success, particularly in its own time. It may be tempting to think of the political theorist in terms of a parallel with the initiator of a new scientific theory, that is, the political equivalent of a Copernicus or Kepler. Engels said of Marx, for example, that his thesis about the economic basis of social organization and development was "destined to do for history what Darwin's theory has done for biology,"[30] and Hobbes believed he might accomplish, regarding the movement of political bodies, what Galileo had achieved in astronomy. Yet although this is often the way the theorist sees himself, this role has been largely reserved for great statesmen, and the theorist has been relegated to playing a largely symbolic part with little impact on those to whom he addressed himself. Although few theorists actually believed in the ultimate likelihood of efficacious involvement in the politics of their day, this ostracism was not easy to accept, since the vision of the theorist is not a passive one.

Enjoined from political action in the ordinary sense, the theorist is satisfied with nothing less than political action in the extraordinary sense, that is, the role of author of a new order shaped in his own image. His impulse is that of the artist to give birth to the vision of symmetry and beauty which grows within him. It usually finds concreteness only in words, but this, nevertheless, tells us something about the literature of political theory and its obsessive concern with beginnings, foundations, and creation. In both the *Republic* and the *Laws,* the interlocutors engage in a foundation play which recounts the rise and decline of political order and results in the appearance of a new order that reflects the dialectical course of their conversation. All political theory constitutes a somewhat similar drama of fall and redemption. For Machiavelli, it is a story which leads from the greatness of Rome to the "extreme misery, infamy, and degradation" of the present and finally to a projection of a united Italy and a reconstructed republic.[31] For Locke and Hobbes it is a movement from a state of nature (historical, hypothetical, symbolic) to the organization of political life under a social contract. For Rousseau, it is a fall from a state of natural grace to a corrupt political society which can be redeemed by a new and properly constituted founding. For Marx a similar path is followed from primitive communism to the future socialist society. In each case, it is a movement from order to chaos to order. It is always, at least symbolically, in part a historical tale, because history is the setting of political creation and decay, and a proper foundation is the secret to overcoming history. The founding tale is always a reconstruction of the beginning or the natural. It is not a return to the natural, which is irretrievably lost, but art copying, purifying, and, at the same time, overcoming nature. Marx's concern with the etiology of social pathology was by no means unique. To found and contain society within the primordial moment of the foundation is a persistent theme in political theory.

Yet the theorist recognizes well the gap between the words of his foundation tale and their realization in political institutions. His estrangement from society is a manifestation of the dilemma of the distance between power and knowledge which obsesses every theorist. For Plato, the prerequisite for founding a just city was that philosophy and kingship be united in one individual, and, like Plato, Rousseau maintains that "so long as power alone is on one side, and knowledge and understanding alone on the other, the learned will seldom make great objects their study, princes will still more rarely do great actions, and the people will continue to be, as they are, mean, corrupt, and miserable."[32] The theorist knows that ultimately philosophers will not be kings and that rulers will continue to "disdain to admit into their councils those who are most capable of giving them good advice."[33] This is in part because the vision of the theorist is too brilliant for society to perceive unmediated.

There is little doubt that Plato saw himself as the true statesman, the person with knowledge even when denied a city in which to act, and so, barred from being a builder, he could hope to be an architect. Machiavelli knew that the theorist must at best settle for a role in which he will "teach others that good which the malignity of the times and of fortune has prevented his doing himself" and that "someone perhaps more favored by Heaven, may perform it."[34] He visualizes himself as the true prince who has both knowledge and proper motives, but he must settle for directing his work towards someone who is "worthy" to govern and has the "desire" but not the "knowledge."[35] Just as Moses required his mouthpiece in Aaron, the theorist requires an agent. The theorist is the link between truth and society, but he in turn requires an intermediary to stand between himself and society. Plato requires his tyrant, Aristotle his statesman, Machiavelli his founding prince, Hobbes his sovereign, Rousseau his legislator, and Marx his party vanguard to transform, in Hobbes's words, the "truth of speculation, into the utility of practice."[36] It should also be noted that the theorist's agent often suffers the same fate, that is, he cannot be part of the new society either. A hero is required, and, like most heroes, his role is ultimately one of sacrifice to the principle he wittingly or unwittingly propagates or institutes. There is no better portrait of the sacrificing hero than Machiavelli's prince who would liberate Italy and perhaps prepare the way for a republican regime in which he would have no place. In every case, the founders and reformers are instruments of the theorist or the truth he advances. Yet the theorist's alienation is not simply the product of the fact that society will not accept him. The theorist realizes that in coming to terms with political matter, any institutionalized form of his vision is far from the truth that he sees with the eye of his soul and ultimately not a place that satisfies the demand of his psyche.

Plato's just city in the *Republic,* the city of the "noble lie," as well as the city in the *Laws,* contain no philosopher nor can they support a philosophical way of life. The philosopher's city in the *Republic* is more than a merely just city; it is a city for gods. Yet it faces the paradox of perfect embodiment and degenerates because it does not come to terms with the requirements of material survival. The point is simply that all political orders rest on illusion, and the theorist as creator, no more than God, has a place in the illusion he creates but necessarily stands outside it. All political theory has a pronounced dramaturgical quality. This is true, not only with regard to the foundation play which characterizes the structure of these works but also in the sense that the theorist is in the position of a script-writer in search of a producer, and, if fortunate, an opportunity to be a director who shapes political actors into a company. Further, the symbol of the drama captures another important dimension of political theory and that is the recognition that the political world is an illusion.

The theorist is a destroyer of illusion, the subversive who seeks to undercut the form and substance of the symbolic crystal of society. Plato attacks not only the political principles and institutions of the polis which have brought Athens to its debased condition but the poetic oral culture grounded in Homer that sustains those values. Hobbes lashes out bitterly against the Aristotelean teaching in the universities that stands in the way of his revisions of the theoretical foundations of political society. It is not, however, that the theorist believes, or even recommends, that the illusions of the past should be replaced by truth, for each knows too well the ultimate incompatibility between truth and politics. The theorist is the creator of a new illusion which he believes expresses knowledge the old did not. Political society cannot bear the truth of order in undiluted form, but it can act out an illusion that expresses the truth of order. The theorist knows well the difficulties of maintaining the illusions of political society but he also knows that it is even more difficult to maintain political society without illusion. If, as Aristotle argued, political science is the master science, the political theorist is the master illusionist.

It is not that the city described in Plato's *Laws* is divinely instituted or actually linked with the rhythm of the cosmos, but that citizens, living under a myth proclaiming the unity of cosmos and society, are taught to think and act in this way. He who sees history as a mirror of cosmic movement, a process of eternal return, will act accordingly and, in effect, negate social change and history by creating an illusion of timelessness through the structuring of political behavior into ritualistic patterns that eliminate the awareness of unique events which support the consciousness of change. Machiavelli's prince works not so much by physical force as by his ability to create and manipulate illusions, and, in the end, Machiavelli's theory of a republic rests on the fact that men can be educated to see the world in a certain way. The social contract, described by Hobbes, Locke, and Rousseau is not so much an explanation of how political society came, or might come, into being, or even a justification of it, as it is an argument that political society must be perceived by the participants, including the rulers, as if it were such a community if order is to be preserved. Like Plato's *Laws,* they provide an ideology for the citizen. And certainly Rousseau's conception of a society where men are "forced to be free" and always see their will as identical with the general will is nothing more than a vision of behavior structured by illusion. Even James Madison learned from his study of the classics that "all governments rest on opinion."[37] To a large extent, Marx's enchanting tales about the stages of society and the inevitability of a socialist community must be seen as precisely that, enchanting tales calculated to provide the basis of a new illusion but now one that is intended to serve reason and save mankind.

But, in the end, is this apparently serious play about restructuring society not a kind of madness? Maybe the motives of the theorists are really not very different from those of a figure such as Newton who confronts a traditional conception of the physical world with a new vision of reality. Yet unlike the great scientist's revolutionary but contemplative view of nature, the political theorist is demanding a new form of political behavior and a new institutional order that reflects his understanding of human being. One might suggest that in science a new conception of some aspect of the world ultimately brings with it a new mode of practicing science and a fundamental change in the constitution of the scientific community, but the theorist seldom has this impact on politics. Although the analogy with science and the conflict between scientific theories may illuminate some elements of the activity of political theory, where it fails is also instructive. The political theorist does not stand to politics as the revolutionary scientist stands to science, because ultimately political theory is a demand for the transformation of political nature. It is more like the case of the artist who in wishing to cleave the stone must first understand its structural qualities. It is more like alchemy than science, more like the work of Frankenstein; it is the impulse not only to understand and manipulate political nature but to transcend it. The impulse is like that of the sculptor in his attempt to impose new form on matter, and Plato as well as Machiavelli realized that like all creative acts this requires doing some violence to the material. Politics is the consequence of human action and is the part of existence that is without intrinsic rhythm and form. The man who first constructed a polis, Aristotle said, was "the greatest of benefactors,"[38] and every theorist realized that in this endeavor man becomes most like a god and comes closest to achieving immortality both in the sense of constituting a social cosmos and in the sense of leaving a memorial of himself behind.

Political theory is a call for a new foundation which is required when everyday political action is no longer effective in sustaining order. What is demanded is a new beginning. Yet to accomplish this, what often seems to be sacrificed in the theorist's vision is reflective political action itself. Both rulers and ruled, and often even founders, must be contained within the ordering myth and the institutional order in such a manner that the unpredictable and random character of individual action is nullified. The theorist is not only pessimistic about the possibilities of creative action in society at a particular time and place where virtue has been weakened, but about the potential of action as such and the possibility of relying on individual men as the saviors of society. From Plato's *Laws* (through Polybius, Machiavelli, Harrington, Montesquieu, and Hume) to the *Federalist Papers* the dream has been to overcome through artifice the uncertain and unique character of human behavior, which is the very stuff of history and politics, by the wisdom of institutions imbued with the knowledge of the theorist at the point of their foundation, just as the uniqueness of events in nature are subsumed in the patterns that God imposed on the world at the beginning. The constitutional vision of a political cosmos bearing the imprint of its author has been a recurring theme in political theory.

Just as Plato, in the *Republic,* found the answer to disorder in the relationship between psyche and city, that is, in the discovery that disordered souls create political chaos and that political chaos in turn releases the springs of disorder in the human soul, every theorist ultimately seeks the answer to political order, and finds the basis of his design, in this same relationship. Every political theory is a venture in the search for the true nature of human being which in one way or another becomes the model of the city whether the city is considered to be, as for Aristotle, a space for moral development or, as for St. Augustine, a dispensation by God for the restraint of sinners. Sometimes the institutions he imagines are ones that would order human behavior through a process of political education and sometimes political institutions are viewed as a cage which would conform to, and control, an unmalleable human nature in such a way as, in Mandeville's words, to create public benefit from private vice. In any event, for the theorist, the problem of creating and sustaining polities is ultimately, as Hobbes maintains, due to a lack of a true science of politics, and thus "the fault is not in men, as they are the *matter;* but as they are the *makers,* and orderers of them."[39]

POLITICAL THEORY
IN THE CONTEMPORARY AGE

A question inevitably arises about the status of political theory today, but it does not deserve a great deal of attention. The question has been answered in a number of ways, but most of the arguments are ultimately unsatisfying since they tend to presuppose the intellectual context of the myth of the tradition. In some respects, the question is no longer meaningful once it is removed from this context, since it was prompted by the problem of whether the tradition had come to an end. If what is taken to constitute the literature of political theory is, as proposed here, simply analytically distinguished in terms of certain family resemblances, then to speak of a beginning, end, and future has little significance. Yet it is still possible to ask if this *kind* of literature, literature which fits the model, is being produced. I would argue that it is not and that to a great extent it must be viewed as a historical artifact, but this does not make it any less valuable as an object of study. Although I believe it is misleading to speak of political theory as a traditional activity which has declined, those individuals such as Strauss, Arendt, and Wolin who have attempted to explain the decline of political theory have probably isolated some of the significant reasons for the demise of this kind of literature. The diffusion of the idea of the political and its disappearance as a distinct object of inquiry; the belief that a search for human nature is futile and the increasing sense that human beings are historical animals or in some way products of their social context; the inversion of the classical priorities of public and private in modern life; and the positivist and historicist attack on claims of transcendental truth are probably all relevant factors in understanding the disengagement of creative thought from the problem of political order. Such reasons are legion, but apart from these considerations, there is one other factor which may suggest doubts about the survival of political theory in the West. This involves the conditions of its production.

There may be an important sense in which the open society and political theory are incompatible. This is not to imply that the open society is necessarily the good society that transcends ideology and stands beyond the need for criticism and the remedial vision of the theorist, but rather that the theorist may be an anachronism in a society marked by conditions of extreme tolerance and the soft despotism of mass society that oppresses by ignoring. Political theory is a heroic venture. It is to have the boldness and arrogance to see into the future, to threaten society with disaster, to proclaim not only that institutional arrangements are in some way wrong but that what seems as real to every man as the furniture of the world, including his vision of himself, is in fact an illusion. It is not only to hold out alternatives but to attempt to undertake their realization. Yet heroes need space in which to act and a mode of activity through which to distinguish themselves. In a society where everyone engages in predicting the future; where there are continual threats of disaster that go far beyond the command of normal comprehension; where the media compress the universe so that the distinctness of the dimensions of time is lost and the significance of events is leveled; where all kinds of extreme social criticism and outrageous speculation, and even bizarre action, become commonplace and are received with little sanction; and where the number of published works condemn almost any written treatise to a short period of recognition, if any, the political theorist is not unlike Sophocles's Ajax, a hero without a field of action or anyone to notice him if he does act.

The open society and the simultaneous contraction, depreciation, and loss of identity of the political or public realm go hand in hand, and thus the conditions of theorizing and the object of theorizing tend to disappear together. A political community is necessarily an exclusive community with definite limits of diversity, but not all social orders are based on political community. What one usually understands as the open society is grounded on the assumption that men find identity in diverse private communities and that the very purpose of the political is to protect and facilitate this pluralism. In other words, the open society and the precedence of private over substantive public ends are mutually supportive ideas, and ideas that are not conducive to political theorizing. This is not to suggest that the kind of impulse that gives rise to political theory has disappeared but only that the vehicle and object of this impulse must be sought elsewhere. It is not likely that the study of the history of political theory will lead to a revival of political theory, but at least it may reawaken a sense of the possibility, or at least the ideal, of a creative reordering or reconstitution of social life.

NOTES

1. For a discussion of Plato in these terms see, John G. Gunnell, *Political Philosophy and Time* (Middletown, Conn.: Wesleyan University Press, 1968).

2. For representative discussions of this subject see Eric Voegelin, *Order and History,* vol. 3, *Plato and Aristotle* (Baton Rouge: Louisiana State University Press, 1957), pp. 304 ff.; Nicholas Lobkowicz, *Theory and Practice: History of a Concept from Aristotle to Marx* (Notre Dame: University of Notre Dame Press, 1967), Chs. 1–4; C. Kerenyi, *The Religion of the Greeks and Romans* (New York: Dutton, 1962), Ch. IV; Peter Euben, "Creatures of a Day: Thought and Action in Thucydides," in Terrence Ball, ed., *Political Theory and Practice: New Perspectives* (Minneapolis: University of Minnesota Press, 1977).

3. Edith Hamilton and Huntington Cairns, eds., *The Collected Dialogues of Plato* (New York: Pantheon Books, 1961), pp. 715, 860.

4. Cicero, *Tusculan Disputations,* trans. J. E. King (Cambridge: Harvard University Press, 1960), p. 433.

5. See Aristotle, *Politics,* VII and *Nichomachean Ethics,* I, X.

6. See Hamilton and Cairns, *The Collected Dialogues of Plato,* pp. 1574–1598.

7. *The Complete Writings of Thucydides: The Peloponnesian War* (New York: Modern Library, 1951), pp. 3, 15.

8. Niccolo Machiavelli, *The Prince* (bound with) *The Discourses,* (New York: Modern Library, 1950), p. 4; *Mandragola* (New York: Bobbs-Merrill, 1957), p. 4.

9. Jean-Jacques Rousseau, *The Social Contract (bound with) Discourses* (New York: Dutton, 1950), p. 3.

10. Thomas Hobbes, *Leviathan* (New York: Collier Books, 1962), p. 511.

11. Hamilton and Cairns, *The Collected Dialogues of Plato,* p. 736; *The Letters of Machiavelli* (New York: Capricorn Books, 1961), p. 249.

12. For a more detailed discussion of this theme, see Gunnell, *Political Philosophy and Time.*

13. *The Politics of Aristotle,* trans. Ernest Barker (Oxford: Clarendon Press, 1946), pp. 5, 7.

14. Machiavelli, *The Prince* (bound with) *The Discourses,* p. 272.

15. Ibid., p. 103.

16. Hobbes, *Leviathan,* p. 30.

17. Ibid., pp. 236, 237, 248.

18. Machiavelli, *The Prince* (bound with) *The Discourses,* p. 397.

19. Rousseau, *Reveries,* quoted in George Poulet, *Studies in Human Time* (New York: Harper & Row, 1959), p. 163.

20. Rousseau, *The Social Contract* (bound with) *Discourses,* pp. 87, 88.

21. Karl Marx and Friedrich Engels, *Basic Writings on Politics and*

Philosophy, ed. Lewis S. Feuer, (New York: Anchor Books, 1959), p. 245.

22. Hamilton and Cairns, *The Collected Dialogues of Plato,* p. 732.

23. Ibid., p. 1605.

24. Ibid., p. 819.

25. Ibid., pp. 732, 1578.

26. Machiavelli, *The Prince* (bound with) *The Discourses,* p. 49.

27. For an analysis of political theory as strategic writing, see Charles D. Tarlton, "The Creation and Maintenance of Governments: A Neglected Dimension of Hobbes's *Leviathan,*" *Political Studies* 26 (1978).

28. Hobbes, *Leviathan,* pp. 248–49, 270.

29. Rousseau, *The Social Contract* (bound with) *Discourses,* p. 144.

30. Marx and Engels, *Basic Writings,* pp. 4–5.

31. Machiavelli, *The Prince* (bound with) *The Discourses,* p. 273.

32. Rousseau, *The Social Contract* (bound with) *Discourses,* p. 174.

33. Ibid., p. 173.

34. Machiavelli, *The Prince* (bound with) *The Discourses,* p. 273.

35. Ibid., p. 102.

36. Hobbes, *Leviathan,* p. 270.

37. *The Federalist,* ed. Jacob E. Cooke (New York: Meridian Books, 1961), p. 340.

38. Aristotle, *Politics,* trans. Ernest Barker (New York: Oxford University Press, 1946), p. 7.

39. Hobbes, *Leviathan,* p. 237.

Index

History of ideas, tradition
of, 22–27, 68
Hobbes, Thomas, 40, 64, 88, 94,
134, 137, 145, 146, 149, 153
abstract character of, 151
on classic tradition, 88, 156
Locke's refutation of, 53
on political authority, 54
and political crisis, 142, 152
quoted, 95
social contract of, 154, 157
and sovereign, 155
Homer, 137, 144, 156
Homo faber, 50
Human sciences. *See also* Social
sciences
interpretation of, 110
philosophy and, 120

Ideas, history of, 22–27, 68, 117
Ideology, critique of, 115–16
Inquiry
historical, 122
theory and practice in, 124
Interpretation. *See also*
Hermeneutics
alternative paradigms of, 117
criteria of, 73
historical, 107
of history of political theory,
126
methodological problems
of, 102–3
philosophy of, 125
process of, 114, 115
theory of, 104
Interpretative analysis, 70
Interpreter, task of, 99
Italy, disunity of, 142

Jaspers, Karl, 80

Kepler, Johannes, 153
Kierkegaard, Sören, 47
Knowledge
enlightenment theories of, 112
and hermeneutics, 106
historical, 107
Kuhn, Thomas, 56, 83, 84, 102,
122, 123

Labor, 48
Language, 120
and interpreter, 105
meaning in, 124
of morals, 9
and thought, 117
universality of, 111
Laslett, Peter, 9
Laws (Plato), 140, 145, 149, 150,
154, 156, 157
Leviathan (Hobbes), 151
Liberalism
intellectual foundations of, 73
intellectual nihilism of, 77
Linguistic analysis, 11
Linguistics
of historical phenomena, 100
meaning in, 119
Literature. *See also* Classic works
and history of ideas, 24
on history of political
theory, 134
on political theory, 89
Locke, John, 40, 55, 149, 152, 154
refutation of Hobbes, 53
social contract of, 157
Logic, of morals, 9

Machiavelli, 1, 53, 54, 69, 132, 134,
137, 141, 142, 149, 154, 155
and classic tradition, 87–88
political philosophy of, 39, 40,
138
representation of, 150
and study of history, 146–47
theory of republic, 157–58
McIlwain, C. H., 5
Easton's criticism of, 17
quoted, 3
Madison, James, 157
Mandeville, Bernard, 1, 59
Mandragola (Machiavelli), 141–42
Marx, Karl, 42, 46, 47, 81, 88, 142,
153, 154, 155
in classic tradition, 68
criticism of, 78, 79
and historical process, 40, 146
and political crisis, 152
and practice in political
science, 148

Marxism, 21, 26, 78
Materialism, in liberal democratic
    society, 45
Meaning, 105
    of historical event, 113
    in language, 124
    political, 53, 54
    and understanding, 118
Mens auctoris, 123
Merriam, Charles E., 15, 16, 17
Metaphysics, tradition of, 81
Methodism, 56–57
Methodological problems, 96
    in hermeneutical theory, 110
    in history of ideas, 24, 101
    of interpretation, 102–3
Mill, John Stuart, 88, 136
Modernity, 40, 69, 74
Montesquieu, Charles de
    Secondat, 55
Moral relativism, 5
Moses, 155

Natural sciences, 120, 121, 122.
    See also Sciences
Newton, Isaac, 157
Nietzsche, Friedrich W., 40, 42,
    46, 47, 81
Nihilism, 38

Oakeshott, Michael, 25
    on history of political
        philosophy, 86
    quoted, 65
Order
    history of, 41
    truth of, 156
Order and History, (Voege-
    lin), 41, 43

Parmenides, 48
Phenomenology, 11
Philistinism, 38
Philosophy
    of history, 12, 76–78
    and human sciences, 120
    of interpretation, 103
    and politics, 149, 154
Plato, 68, 69, 130, 134, 142, 147,
    149, 150, 155, 156, 158

architectonic view of, 148
Arendt on, 47, 48, 79
in classic tradition, 11, 37, 41,
    87, 88, 137
dialogue on Socrates, 140
Heidegger on, 81
historical view of, 144
philosopher's city of, 75, 154
on role of philosopher, 153
Pluralism, Western, 20
Pocock, J.G.A., 99, 100, 101, 103
    and history of ideas, 119
    and paradigm change, 102
Poiesis, 49
Polis
    Aristotle on, 145, 158, 159
    classical, 48
Political crises
    and classic works, 142–43
    modern, 73
Political ideas, tradition of, 19. *See
    also* History
Political order, radical autonomy
    of, 54
Political philosophy, 9
    classical, 36–40
    decline of, 54
    history of, 40, 48
Political science
    American, 21
    behavioralism of, 97
    empirical, 14
    new revolution in, 10
    old and new, 22
    and political theory, 4–11
    in West, 15
Political theory
    as academic discipline, 90
    in contemporary age, 159–61
    decline of, 4–11
    derailment of, 40–46
    "Great Books" approach to, 6
    great tradition of, 71
    of Greeks, 15
    history of, 12–22, 52, 55,
        125–56
    and history of ideas, 22–27
    literature of, 159–60
    Plato, 137
    propositions in, 20
    and scientific method, 7